AF253279

DISCOGRAPHY

Psychostick
DO (2018)
Revenge of the Vengeance (2014)
Space Vampires vs. Zombie Dinosaurs in 3D (2011)
The Digital Appetizer (2010)
Sandwich (2009)
The Flesh Eating Rollerskate Holiday Joyride (2007)
We Couldn't Think of a Title (2003)
Die…a LOT! – Demo (2001)
Don't Bitch, it's Free – Demo (2000)

Debtors
Debtors (2018)

Evacuate Chicago
Veracity (2010)

The Stuttering C-Cowboys
Various songs recorded from 2004-2006

Praise for *Dichotomies*

"A remarkable first-person odyssey of a young touring musician who artfully combines his comedy rock music performances with completing demanding, long distance, higher education studies. Dontre offers a living, often humorous, and sometimes bawdy, chronicle of memorable characters he meets on the road. He adds to the mix practical insights gleaned from his school work, as well as vivid descriptions of the highly-charged, emotional ups and downs of high energy concert work."

-Ray Forbes, Ph.D., Chair, M.S. in Business Psychology, Franklin University

"I feel stuck between a rock and a hard place and cannot decide if this book is funny or insightful. As inferred from its title, that's probably because it is both."

-Mats E. Eriksson, Ph.D., author of *Another Primordial Day*, Professor of Paleontology, Lund University

"This is a must-read for any potential college student who thinks that they can't do it, whatever the reason. 'I'm not the college type…I'm too (fill in the blank…).' Alex shows that with some tenacity and grit, anyone really can earn a degree—even on the road and next to a dumpster! I am truly in awe of what he accomplished and how he stayed committed to this amazing journey. It is the rare student that can expose a professor to a new iteration of a genre of music while also contributing to the field of business psychology in a meaningful way. After 20 years of teaching, Alex has motivated me to work harder to be a source of motivation to my future students."

-Kristan Jones, Ph.D., Professor of Business Psychology, Franklin University, Director of HR Talent Development at Raymond James

"On tour, while the rest of us were crapping, napping, fapping or gormandizing, Alex was studying and working on speeches for his degree. It doesn't end there, then he would play a flawless set every night on the drums…he's a bad-ass dude with a heart of gold."

-**Todd Smith,** Dog Fashion Disco, Polkadot Cadaver, & Knives Out

"I can't really say whether human psychology and touring go hand in hand, or if they are arch enemies…but I will never forget walking off a soundcheck to find Alex's face lit by his laptop while working on a psychology paper. Usually the few times I have seen people whip out laptops on tour is to pay their bills, Skype with the family, or to check in with their probation officers, and not to write academic articles on "Psychology of Organizational Coaching". To pull things like that off in a touring environment is as impressive as the drumming of Alex Dontre."

-**Niklas Karvonen, Ph.D.,** Machinae Supremacy, CTO of Substorm

"Every touring musician understands the difficulty of maintaining a life on the road and a life back at home. Alex decided to do both at the same time, and I'm not sure if that makes him brilliant or deranged."

-**Daniel Drinnen, M.A.,** URIZEN

"Sex, drugs, and rock and roll is a tired cliché. Alex is a perfect example of a man with concrete goals, willing to utilize technology and time management to plan for his future. Witnessing his dedication and work ethic every day on tour definitely made me wonder if I should be doing something more with my life."

-**Neil Patterson,** Downtown Brown

DICHOTOMIES

Lessons from a College Life on Tour

Alex Dontre

10% of the proceeds to go to the 1902 Leadership Circle Scholarship and the Columbus State Community College Foundation in equal amounts. Without scholarships, this book would not exist. Let's help fund the next educational story.

First Printing: 2019

ISBN: 978-0-359-99378-9

Psychostick
2328 E. Lincoln Hwy #232
New Lenox, IL 60451
http://psychostick.com

Feel free to join me on Goodreads:
www.goodreads.com/author/show/19722610.Alex_Dontre

DEDICATION

To my loving partner, Lora, whose support of this project remains unwavering despite meeting me a month after the story concludes.

CONTENTS

ACKNOWLEDGMENTS

Huge thanks to my band & tour mates from 2011-2017: Robert Kersey, Josh Key, Matty J "Moose", Patrick "Murph" Murphy, Matt "Kooks" Kuchta, Tony Schiavo, Rob "Manny" Whisenhunt, Jesse "Turff" McInturff, Elliot Mapes, Nolan McCormick, Billy Rymer, Chris Stockton, Emerson Moorhead, Dan DeFonce, John the bus driver, Frieda Geiger, Mushroomhead, Ventana, Screaming Mechanical Brain, Downtown Brown, Black Light Burns, Dog Fashion Disco, Polkadot Cadaver, American Head Charge, Nekrogoblikon, URIZEN, Ideamen, Danimal Cannon, Machinae Supremacy, One-Eyed Doll, Wolfborne, Hed PE, & the many hundreds of friends & family members who let us sleep in your homes without complaining.

To my wonderful professors: Beth Barnett, Ronald Devera, Brad Trimble, Gordon Brookhart, Lee Wayard, Norm Hicks, Mingzhi Xu, Don Bruce, Mark Jackson, Jill Cadotte, Sallone Asiamah, Tracy Shroyer, Glenn Clayman, Amy DiBlasi, Mary Vaughn, Deborah Hoffman, Jack Popovich, Mark Polifroni, Michelle Duda, Lauren Thomas, Bethany Poore, Miriam Abbott, Anjali Gupta, Amy Eaton, Terry Skiba, Bryan Grady, Nancy Fidler, Mark Massen, Sandra Gresham, Jack Groseclose, Clay Benton, Edgar Velez, Kevin Doll, Merideth Sellars, Ted O'Flaherty, Paul Sweeney, Diane Alexander, Jeffrey Ferezan, George Redmond, John Moore, Pamala Ratvasky, Steve Whatley, Lydia Gilmore, Ted Jones, Kristan Jones, & Anne Soltysiak.

To the excellent CSCC & Franklin University faculty & staff: Sandra Veach, Denise Cashon, Laura Baisden, Erika Hill, Regina Harper, Cathy Giles, David Kerr, Jessica Lickeri, Tracy Austin, Sarah Hyatt, Jonathan Morton, Martina Peng, Bruce Campbell, Kevin Greenwood, Sharon Massen, Erin Glass, Todd Hampel, Aaron Cassady, Merchel Menefield, Sara Burris, Stephanie Hicks, Brian Petereit, Alyssa Darden, David Harrison, Brenda Jones, Ray Forbes, Kelly Renner, Denver Fowler, Christopher Washington, & David Decker.

To the out-of-state proctor testing staff: Jennifer Arth, Ted Bartke, Christine Danish, Terry Pease, Jeremy Worrell, Linda Anderson, Joan Nicely, Shelly Trujillo, Noreen Wade, & Carrie Wolf.

To others who graciously helped me succeed: Paul & Jessica Berick, Sarah & Cameron Groff, Mark & Leslie Harris, Nick & Jen Church, Jen Kuchta, Laura Johnson-LeDeux & family, Aljon Inertia, Mats E. Eriksson, Niklas Karvonen, Todd Smith, Neil Patterson, Magda Ksiazak, Mindee Silva, Shannon Murphy, Hope Stockton, Trish Malloy, Terry Thompson, Paul & Heather Truitt, Sarah Hagan, Steve Lobmeier, Rachel Wang, Linda Shinn, Wyatt Christman, Ashley Nutini, Catherine Giles, Aaron McComb, Kodi Temes, the lovely Lora Kennedy, & lastly, Travis Barker & Dessa for writing outstanding books about tour life (not to mention the awesome music).

Finally, to everyone who attended the 505 Psychostick shows from September 2011 to May 2017.

PREFACE

I am not a rock star; I'm a musician. In my view, rock stars are those people you only read about in books or observe with astonishment in documentaries. To be fair, I've met a few. They are often insufferable humans with few redeemable qualities save their musical skills.

Thus, this is not a tale of a "rock star" life of drugs and sex and partying all night. This is a book about my struggles and triumphs as a college student while touring with my band, Psychostick. Specifically, I am the drummer of said band, and we've been going strong since 2000 when I met Josh and Rob for the first time at age 15, and Matty a decade and many adventures later in 2010.

In case you're new to the Psychostick camp, allow me to introduce everyone. Rob Kersey is our vocalist and web designer. Josh Key is our guitarist and audio engineer. Matty J "Moose" is our bass player and merch extraordinaire. Our other Matt, who goes by Matt "Kooks" Kuchta, is our hotshot video star and also the "anything you can imagine" technician. Need a blood cannon? Ask Kooks. Finally, Patrick "Murph" Murphy is our video director and secret weapon. He helps write a lot of the lyrics, especially on the more recent albums. Your cordial author is the drummer and tour manager.

My intention in writing this book is not to pore over my reasons for enrolling in college post break up. Granted, 2011 was quite an emotionally challenging year as I pieced my life back together following a relationship with a wonderful woman who is now married to an equally wonderful guy. Fortunately, I have salvaged my friendship with both, and we still convene from time to time when I visit Columbus.

That said, the primary reason for enrolling in my first classes in late 2011 was a desire for an autonomous bit of achievement. Until then, all my triumphs had been part of a team, whether it was as a member of a band or a member in a relationship. I had also recognized a huge deficit in my knowledge and skills with financial matters. Accordingly, I enrolled in my first finance class with no intention to continue further. Carry on to learn more about my bizarre life.

INTRODUCTION TO TOUR LIFE

The floor was alive with ants thriving on Honey Nut Cheerios. It was not an ideal place to rest, despite our severe exhaustion of being four weeks into a tour and not even at the half-way point. All I wanted to do was sleep, especially after the night we had. Psychostick was the opening act for the 2010 Nashville Pussy and Green Jellÿ tour, and before our set, we learned that no one was going to be paid by the promoter. As an extended (and likely heated) argument ensued outside, we opted to go ahead and perform anyway. We didn't get into this business to drive 700 kilometers[1] from Des Moines to leave our fans in the lurch.

Accordingly, Tulsa received our performance as the only touring band to play that night, and we were subsequently chewed out by the tour manager (known as a "TM") for "giving up our power" to get paid. In the end, we opted to set

---

[1] Of nearly 200 countries in the world, only three refuse to use the metric system.

up our merch in the parking lot outside and were able to earn some gas money to make it to the following night's show in San Antonio.

Back in the aptly named "living room" of the house with the writhing ants, I dismally realized I would be spending yet another night in the sweltering van. The couple who offered to house us for the evening were friendly enough, but hygiene did not seem to be their familial priority. As the wife proceeded to ignite the stove to prepare a late-night snack, I sheepishly asked to use the shower. If nothing else, I could at least clean myself, if not their infested carpet.

With my clothes in hand, I once again entered the homely anthill. I had been given directions to the master bedroom's shower because it was in "better condition." That sounded fine to me, so I made my way to the hallway as instructed. I had to pause for a moment to comprehend that I would need to surmount a pile of clothing up to my waist to gain access to the intended bedroom. With a quick hop, I was in the room and immediately froze in alarm. There was a second, full-grown woman asleep in the bed. While I'm not one to judge others' life choices, I was perturbed with the idea of this woman waking to see a strange, exhausted man sneaking past her.

Fortunately, she remained deep in slumber and I continued on unabated. As I triumphantly entered the bathroom, I gazed upon something unimaginable. A baby's used diaper was stuck to the tile, poop down, adjacent to the toilet. I steadied myself after a moment of shock and proceeded to glance around. There it was, even more unconscionable than the diaper—an empty Snickers wrapper. What kind of monster eats a candy bar in a room with a dirty diaper stuck to the floor?

Determined to overcome this horror of a night, I quickly

found a relatively clean spot on the sink to rest my clothing as I showered. If I could not wash myself of the memory, I would at least wash my body. I anxiously tip-toed to the shower, careful to avoid any other land mines, no doubt with a grimace on my face. Finally, I was able to pull the knob to invite the water to wash away my agitation from the preceding several minutes.

Rather than flow out into the tub below, the leaky shower head blasted me directly in my right eye with Arctic water. Involuntarily, my body leaped backward, and the frigid torrent soaked my once dry clothes. I only later realized that the shower head was the singular reason there was even a clean spot at all.

CHAPTER 2011

"What the *fuck* are you doing?" This was the first time someone had asked about my new collegiate touring routine. It was day two of the Slaughterhouse Roadshow, a five-week U.S. run in Autumn. My band Psychostick was direct support for the group Mushroomhead, and we were booked to play all over the East Coast and Midwest. I had begun my first semester[1] at Columbus State Community College (CSCC) just the week before, and I had no intention to neglect my homework just because I was on tour again.

As it turns out, rock venues are not an ideal locale for studying. However, there weren't many options from which to choose. I had perched up in a semi-secluded corner of the venue we were playing that night, a place called Streeters in Traverse City, Michigan. Just the week before, I had begun my

---

[1] CSCC switched from quarters to semesters in 2012, but for simplicity let's just call them all semesters.

college career with two classes, Pre-Algebra and Personal Finance for my first semester, and I was struggling to focus somewhat while Mushroomhead was sound checking. I had purchased a set of Sony noise-canceling headphones along with my textbooks, but they blocked out about as much sound as can be expected from foam cushions barely a centimeter thick.

During sound check, the headliner for the evening typically bangs on each instrument while the sound guy (or sound technician if the person is feeling fancy) dials in the tones and volumes desired. As the band clamored on, a member of the tour party I hadn't yet met stumbled over my laptop's power cable and unplugged my computer. Not at all ideal.

After sound check, I was finally building some momentum with the assignment when I received the profane inquiry from a then-unidentified[2] member of the headlining band regarding my current task. I mumbled something about online classes hoping to discourage the inquisitor from forcing further conversation. Mercifully, the exchange ended abruptly and permitted me to venture on.

Touring is not unlike a semester of university courses, but a tour is perhaps a bit less civilized and more erratic. It is all-encompassing for several weeks, then you move on to the next project. While classes are typically aligned with the seasons and last for the duration of a semester, a given tour might last a couple of weeks or could drag on for several months. By the end of each, all you want is to complete the final exam (or the final show) without bombing and collapse into hibernation.

This tour, however, was just getting started. We had about one day scheduled off per week, so planning ahead was

---

[2] It can be a challenge to learn all the names of a tour party. This is especially true when the band wears masks on stage, like Mushroomhead.

paramount. My exams were of particular concern. Fortunately, the due dates for exams 1 and 2 of my Personal Finance course aligned quite well with the scheduled tour routing. As we had several shows booked in and around Ohio (Mushroomhead's home state), I was able to coordinate visits to the CSCC Testing Center before multiple-hour drives to Lexington and Cleveland, respectively.

The coming weeks would bring a new ritual to the tour routine. Whenever an exam was scheduled, several of my new tour mates would inquire about the material being covered and the testing logistics. Their encouragement prior to the examinations and congratulations after began to cultivate a sense of great appreciation in me. While it was an exclusive new responsibility I had accepted, it became a shared adventure.

Pestering Mushroomhead

Some four weeks into the tour brought us to Dallas at an interesting venue appropriately known as Trees. Rather than humdrum steel support beams to shoulder the roof, the venue features—you guessed it—various tree trunks throughout the building. In fact, one is even located on stage right[3]. It offers a unique indoor experience, although I am suspicious that the trees are in fact fabricated and not living botanic beams immune from the need for electromagnetic radiation and liquid water. The Dallas County Fire Marshal would likely find the whole framework problematic.

It was also the completion of my 27th orbit around Sol, (or simply my birthday if you prefer). Following a notably energetic show, several of my tour mates were eagerly

---

[3] Stage-right and left are from the band's perspective facing the audience.

supplying me with Jäger[4] bombs in an apparent attempt to encourage me to say something inappropriate. Frowning at probably the third plastic cup thrust into my hand, I recall eloquently elucidating the fact that I am not a fan of guzzling drinks in a single enormous gulp like an aquatic bird with a massive gullet.

Evidently, my peers remember this conversation somewhat differently. Probably closer to the truth is the story that I abruptly shouted, "I'm not a goddamn pelican!" Following my nonsensical outburst about water birds, the group began to roar with laughter. None of us may remember the setlist from the concert that evening, but no one will soon forget my heartfelt howl lamenting my commitment to consume another Jäger bomb.

Later that evening, I found myself in a scenario that could have easily gotten my band ousted from the remainder of the tour. To be clear, under no circumstances is it appropriate to bang on the door of the headliner's tour bus. A bus is typically a rental, and a large one featuring 12-15 bunks may cost anywhere between $1,000-1,500 *each day*, regardless if you have a show booked to make money or not. The price tag covers the vehicle, the trailer, the insurance, the driver fees, and whatever else may come with it. Accordingly, the Mushroomhead bus likely cost the band between $40- to $60,000 for the tour. You don't "bang" on a 60-thousand-dollar door.

Regardless, that is exactly what I did. Rick Thomas, a member of the band (and also the TM), promptly swung open the door to see me scowling at him. "You!" Immediately professional, Rick enquired, "What's the problem?" as he

---

[4] A "Jäger bomb" is a syrupy mixture of Jägermeister and an energy drink. Incidentally, the first song I ever wrote for Psychostick was Jagermeister Love Song.

stepped out onto the sidewalk. Without hesitating, I seized the tour laminate hanging from my key ring and held it up to his face. "*This* is the problem. These laminates are WRONG!"

I genuinely wish I could have witnessed the horrified faces of my tour mates as I harassed Rick on the sidewalk in downtown Dallas. Fortunately, he had the sober acumen to recognize that I was being entirely ridiculous with my critical affront regarding erroneous tour dates. If I were a gambler, I would wager that every tour ever booked in history bears at least one inaccurate tour date listed. It is an inescapable fact that as soon as you print the laminates, tour shirts, and promo posters, at least one of the dates will be changed or canceled. In our case it was a show in Hillsdale, Michigan the following week that had been dropped subsequent to the printing process. With an almost imperceptible smirk, Rick brushed off my grievance and returned to his infinitely more amicable bus.

Evidently, my laminate faux pas was not enough to provoke Rick to decide that he hated us. Instead, he invited Psychostick to join him on tour with his other band, Ventana (also performing on the current tour) the following January for another five-week run. How do you brand a tour with such a lineup? In probably the shortest tour name discussion in history, someone unexpectedly blurted out, "How about…the 'Punch Your Cock In' tour?" Rick's response? "Done."

Proctor Exams

Like it or not, exams are a part of college life. It does not matter whether or not you have other obligations. As a student, I had committed to fulfilling the requirements of my two classes. As the Mushroomhead tour came to an end in Missouri and we said goodbye to our new friends, I had one more challenge to overcome.

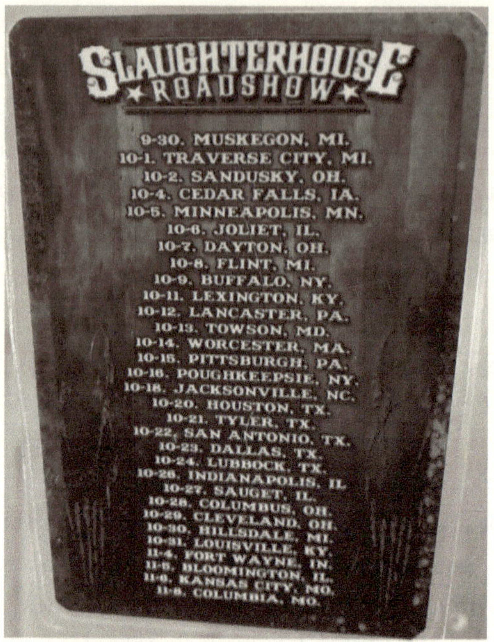

The clearly erroneous tour laminate.

When taking an exam on one's own college or university campus, the requirements are very simple. All you need to do is arrive at the testing center during open hours and complete the assignment prior to the due date. Off-campus proctor exams[5], on the other hand, are a different beast entirely.

My first proctor exam was scheduled the day after our final show on tour. We had stayed with our friends Nick and Jen roughly 20 minutes east of Kansas City in a small suburb known as Grain Valley, Missouri. That morning I borrowed the van while everyone else was still asleep and drove to a local community college to try my luck.

There is a specific protocol to follow if a student wishes to proctor an exam away from one's home college campus. To

---

[5] This is sometimes called remote testing.

explain, proctoring an exam off-site requires the approval of several entities. These include the professor of the course, the student's college or university testing center, and the desired location's testing center (usually another college). Additionally, a touring band member who is also a student must coordinate with fellow bandmates to successfully carry out the mission.

The first exam to be proctored was the second test for my Pre-Algebra class. Months before, I had scoured the area for a suitable location and discovered the Metropolitan Community College - Blue River (MCC-Blue River) campus about 15 minutes from the house. It seemed like a prime testing site, partly because it was a community college rather than an intimidating four-year university.

This is where it gets a bit complex. To uphold the academic standards as an accredited institution, CSCC requires that a student who wishes to have an exam proctored needs to fill out the official Remote Testing Request Form for each exam to be taken off-campus. The application also requires written consent from the professor teaching the class, as well as written consent from the desired proctor site. After requesting permission from my professor (which was granted), then requesting permission from the CSCC Testing Center (granted upon approval from the proctor site), I contacted the MCC-Blue River testing staff.

Once it was all approved, CSCC physically mailed my Pre-Algebra exam directly to the proctor site to await my arrival at MCC-Blue River in November. While it all seemed unnecessarily bureaucratic at first, I soon came to recognize that the numerous careful procedures were indeed an important element of maintaining academic integrity. So be it. I paid my $20 test fee (a written check was required) upon arrival and got to it.

Upon returning to Nick and Jen's home came excited questions about how everything went and how I did. I was pleased to report a successful first proctor experience, with more likely to come in the near future. I still had four exams to go for the term, but I was able to return to Columbus to stay with my ever-gracious friends, Paul and Jessica. I could then take the remainder of my exams on the CSCC campus with fewer hurdles to overcome.

I completed the semester intact. In fact, the two A's I was awarded for my efforts were very encouraging (and much better than my mediocre high school performance). If I could juggle two classes with an extensive tour schedule, what else could I do? Although it was not originally my intention to continue taking classes, I opted for three the following January. My initial finance course had offered a compelling glimpse into the complex realm of investing. I was gradually beginning to realize that you can spend your entire life working for money, or you can make your money work for you.

Personal Finance 101

As the saying goes, "the poor stay poor while the rich get richer." Obviously, this is wildly oversimplified. However, there is some truth to the statement, regardless if the world is not binary, as it is inferred. Then why do the poor stay poor? How do the rich get richer? It's all a matter of simple math. Well, it can be simple, or it can get as complex as you want it to be. For our purposes, let's just keep it easy and pretend that the world is a binary place.

Most people like to buy *stuff*. When I say stuff, I mean that people buy new furniture, TVs, cars, appliances, daily lattes[6]

---

[6] Coffee was the big one for me, and I had no idea. I was purchasing $5 coffees every day. That's about $150/month. It's also $1,825/year. Yikes.

and all kinds of things that lose value over time. Obviously, wealthy people buy stuff too, but they have a different priority. Their priority is to pay *themselves* rather than pay other people by buying stuff. By "pay themselves," I mean they prioritize paying their future selves by putting a significant portion of their income into *owning* companies instead of buying things *from* companies.

Many people think that purchasing a house is an optimal investment because they believe it will continually grow in value. In itself, this is a huge fallacy. Buying a house and expecting it to grow into a retirement plan is a massive risk. All your accumulated wealth is locked up in one singular investment. What happens if your investment floods, or there is a fire, or a tornado, or an earthquake? Insurance is useful, of course, but what might that do to your imagined long-term retirement if your house is no longer worth what you hoped it would be? Or what if the housing market begins to tank like it did in 2007? It puts all your eggs into one basket rather than spreading them out with diversification.

Instead, the simplest way to be a partial owner of a company is to open an account with a financial firm known as a brokerage account. It's kind of like any regular checking or savings account, except you can purchase shares of stock. Shares of stock = literal fractions of ownership. So, owning 100 shares of a company that has 10,000 shares available on the market means that the person would literally own 1% of the company. In reality, most large companies have many millions of shares available, but we're keeping it simple.

It is critical to comprehend the difference in numbers here.

If the average growth of the U.S.[7] economy as a whole is, let's say, 7% per year, that means the money that investors put into buying shares of stock is growing at an average of 7% year after year. Meanwhile, people who only buy *stuff* are losing value because their accumulated wealth is in the form of stuff that depreciates over time. You can think of stuff as a non-productive asset. Sure, it's cool to have a brand-new TV that dwarfs your friend's TV, but it loses value over time as electronics manufacturers release increasingly fancier products. Instead, you could own something that tends to grow in value.

Naturally, there are a couple of caveats here. The first is an economic feature called inflation. This just means that the value of money itself typically shrinks over time. In recent years, average inflation has been around 2%. This is another reason why many people remain poor. A great many people are thrilled when they receive a 2% raise from their jobs each year. However, that 2% raise is in nominal numbers; we want *real* value. So, a 2% raise minus 2% in value loss due to inflation means you are in exactly the same spot as you were the previous year. This is called the money illusion. It also means that the 7% annual growth of the stock market should really be thought of as only 5% because the value of currency declines each year.

The other caveat is taxes. As long as we prefer not to live in a prison cell, we have to pay taxes. So that brokerage account is subject to taxes, just like income earned at a job. However, there is a way to accumulate and grow wealth in a way that isn't reduced by taxes nearly as much. Rather than open a brokerage

---

[7] I enrolled in finance courses in the U.S., thus my use of U.S. companies, economics, and laws. Many other countries have similar financial products, just with different names.

account to buy stock, you can contribute to a retirement plan[8], which is tax-sheltered. In the U.S., this is called an Individual Retirement Account (IRA). You still have to pay taxes on income, however; that is unavoidable.

Now, IRAs come in two basic forms: Traditional IRAs (pay taxes on growth later) and Roth IRAs (pay taxes now). Which is better? There are lots of competing ideas about this, but this is how I see it. Which one offers you a better deal in the long run? What I mean is, when will tax rates likely be lower? Considering the many trillions of dollars of national debt the government has accumulated over the years, I'm banking on taxes going up over time. Thus, I have a Roth IRA to get my taxes out of the way.

If you are unsure of which stocks to purchase, there is a wonderfully simple way to invest responsibly that takes the guessing out of it. There is a financial product called a mutual fund, which is pretty much what it sounds like. It's an investment fund that a whole bunch of individuals mutually put their money into and allow it to grow. Again, we want diversity, not single companies (or houses). Single stocks fluctuate in price much more than a collection of many hundreds of stocks inside a mutual fund. Plus, it catches a much wider net and exposes you to companies of different sizes, different industries, different countries, and so on. When one company tanks, another might skyrocket, and your mutual fund investment is far more protected than just a single company's stock.

Sometimes I hear about how risky it is to invest in the stock market. Do you panic whenever your favorite department

---

[8] Contributing to a 401(k) is an even better option because of employer matching. If you have one, you can max it out first to get the free money and *then* contribute to an IRA.

store puts appliances on sale? Do you rush over to your neighbor's house to try to sell them your current refrigerator, just in case its perceived value that day gets too low for you to be able to sell it tomorrow? Of course not. That would be silly. But that is exactly what far too many people do when the stock market dips down a bit on a "bad" day. Who cares what the stock market does today? The only thing that matters is what the value of your investment ends up looking like decades from now.

I did not fully comprehend all of this by the end of my first semester in college. It was an entirely new assortment of concepts for me. Consider that fact. Why is it that as a society we neglect to teach children the one thing that could mitigate paycheck-to-paycheck thinking and diminish their ongoing financial struggles? Regardless of your desired occupation or calling in life, everyone needs to be comfortable with basic financial concepts. We should teach this in high school, not just in college. It should be a required course when seniors are approaching graduation.

Imagine two students in identical situations. Both are 18 and getting ready to finish high school. Both are working for minimum wage at some terrible fast food joint. However, one of these students enrolls in a finance class and learns not to simply spend every dollar earned on buying *stuff* and instead purchases shares of company ownership in a mutual fund. It accumulates and grows for 30 or 40 or 50 years. That single class could completely transform the life of that student. That's exactly how I felt as I completed my first semester— transformed.

CHAPTER 2012

They had *one job*. All the proctor site needed to do was hold onto my Beginning Algebra exam until the testing day. Instead, they *lost* it. I had organized this whole testing circus weeks ago and even committed to taking it a bit early so I didn't have to worry about it while I was on the road. I was also working diligently with my bass player, Matty, to fully comprehend the material[1]. If it wasn't enough pressure already, having my test magically disappear was an effective way to multiply the intensity.

I explained to the testing site representative (as calmly as I could manage) that there was simply no way I could come back another day once they recovered my exam. We were scheduled to depart for the Ventana tour the following day, and their

---

[1] Matty has a B.S. in Mechanical Engineering from UMass Lowell and was a supremely helpful math tutor on numerous occasions. Even when I got a correct answer, he would often help me understand a more intuitive or more efficient way to think about the problem.

incredible incompetence was not about to wreck my progress.

As the textbook definition of a "non-traditional student," I have developed many creative ways in which to realize my goals. Admittedly, in this case, I utilized a few manipulative ploys to persuade the testing site rep to fix the issue promptly. For instance, I consciously allowed my eye contact to linger a bit longer than is socially acceptable after suggesting we contact CSCC to identify a solution. My posture was also a bit too forward for comfort. I wore a fraudulent smile on my face but at no time raised my voice or uttered any remarks I would regret. Instead, I subtly used body language to help her comprehend that the organizational ineptitude displayed was entirely unacceptable. In the end, we managed to reach the CSCC testing center on the phone, whose wonderful staff agreed to bend the rules and email a digital copy of the exam to the proctor site for them to print out.

That was the last time I ever set foot on that campus. Instead, I found another proctor site in the vicinity at Park University, which has a testing center embedded in a carved-out hill known as the "academic underground." That's one way to discourage cheating. Eliminate cell phone signals from entering the building by burying it under a bed of rock.

Ventana Punches Your Cock In

Much like the Mushroomhead tour, the Punch Your Cock In tour with Ventana was full of rowdy shows in the Midwest and East Coast. I suppose the idea was to revisit many of the same markets recently played a few months before. By then I was a bit more comfortable with the idea of juggling my schoolwork with tour responsibilities and decided to enroll in three simultaneous classes: Beginning Algebra, Financial Accounting, and my second finance course, Investments.

I was particularly interested in the Investments class, as my studies had introduced me to the concept of compound interest. Albert Einstein purportedly once quipped, "Compound interest is the 8th wonder of the world." Another variation often attributed to Einstein is, "The most powerful force in the Universe is compound interest." Variations on a quote (with no listed source) attributed to the same individual do not offer an especially convincing case. Thus, I suspect that both quotes are misattributed to him, although the concept is sound. In any case, study Einstein for theoretical physics; look to Warren Buffett for investing.

As the tour pressed on, I managed to schedule three exams on a single day—one for each class. There was a gap in our tour schedule, the sole day off that week between shows in Battle Creek, Michigan and South Barrington, Illinois. Accordingly, I discovered Moraine Valley Community College in a nearby Chicago suburb. The testing center was easy to find, quiet, comfortable, and most importantly, it seemed professional. I would come to proctor numerous exams at this location in the coming years. Additionally, it cost me just $16 per exam, which seemed like a good deal because it was less than the $20 to which I had previously been anchored[2].

Fortunately, I got through the entire Ventana tour without providing additional evidence that I was a complete lunatic. Granted, there were a few bizarre situations (as with any tour), such as one venue which was already unlocked upon our arrival. No one was in the building, so we began loading in without permission. The "stage" was little more than a few

---

[2] The anchoring effect is a behavioral heuristic I would later study with much enthusiasm. Developed by Amos Tversky and Daniel Kahneman in the 1970s, it describes the tendency of an initial exposure to influence subsequent judgments. This is why a t-shirt marked down from $25 to $20 seems like a good deal, even though $20 might already be the market price.

boards balanced on a foundation of pallets, and the ceiling was low enough to inflict brain damage in the event that someone jumped too enthusiastically. During Ventana's set, the "sound guy," who was apparently not equipped with sufficient expertise to operate the equipment, nearly provoked a brawl with the band members while they were performing. I won't get into specifics as I was not in the room at that moment, but the spirited tales of idiocy combined with supreme overconfidence were entertaining, to say the least.

West Coast with Downtown Brown

A week-long tour with a band one admires is hardly enough. This was the case with our friends in the extraordinary group, Screaming Mechanical Brain, in late April. It was over before we were ready, but fortunately, we had another run lined up beginning just three days later with our friends in Downtown Brown (DTB). They had a wild reputation when I first met them a few years earlier, but I quickly learned that they are some of the kindest and invariably entertaining humans I have ever met[3].

The tour routing took us in a direction we do not often travel due to the high cost of fuel, painfully long drives, and dreaded trailer maintenance[4]. Additionally, 2/3rds of the U.S. population lives in the east half of the country if you slice it right down the middle. However, California is the country's most populous state, so neglecting it entirely isn't wise. In any case, the tour routing brought us across the Rocky Mountains, down the West Coast from Seattle to San Diego, and all the

---

[3] I recently calculated that Psychostick has performed a full 10% of its shows with DTB. With well over 1,200 shows to date, this doesn't simply happen by accident.
[4] I'm not a superstitious person, but if I ever develop a belief in black magic or incantation, it would surely relate to that goddamn devil trailer.

way back to the central region of the country.

By then I was enrolled in three new courses. This time it was English Composition, Beginning Algebra II, and Managerial Accounting. While Managerial Accounting might seem like an extension onto Financial Accounting, there is, in fact, a difference. Financial Accounting includes public financial statements that most people imagine when pondering accounting. This includes balance sheets (the snapshot of the company's status at a specific time, usually the end of the year), the income statement (which illustrates the company's financial performance over a given time), and a cash flow statement. The last one does exactly what the name suggests; it indicates exactly how much cash is coming in and going out.

Meanwhile, Managerial Accounting is concerned with internal procedures, so most people never hear about it. One professor described Managerial Accounting as looking forward through a car's windshield to see where you're going, while Financial Accounting is like peering at your rear-view mirror to see where you have been. Just don't stare into your rear-view mirror too long while you're driving.

If the accounting classes were a bit analytical for my taste, the English course made up for it by offering me a chance to espouse my creativity. Each student was to choose a controversial theme to research and write about for the duration of the semester. Don Bruce, our professor for the course, maintained an interesting perspective that I quickly learned to appreciate. If you put in the work, he will do anything he can to help you. If not, well, why are you here?

The only constant in the Universe is change[5]. One obvious

---

[5] This is a turn of phrase, not a literal statement. If you're a physicist, I'm not arguing against things like Planck's constant or the speed of light. Please resist the urge to send me hate mail.

example of this is technology. Thus, I chose to write about Internet piracy for my controversial theme. I thought it would make a compelling subject, especially since I decided to argue in favor of it, despite the prevailing attitude of the music industry since the dawn of the new millennium. While many bands prefer to grumble and lament about the "good old days" when people used to buy more physical music, my camp never bought into the hype.

Music lovers are listening to more music than ever, but it's up to the artists to offer compelling tangible packages if they want to sell physical music. Nine Inch Nails and Tool are great examples of artists who understand this. Bands who cut costs by selling CDs in cheap, flimsy cardboard sleeves with no additional art, liner notes, or lyrics are perpetuating the issue. No one wants to feel ripped off.

In any case, I knew a good amount about the subject already and thought it would be interesting for my professor to read papers in favor of piracy in a world that almost universally condemns it. Plus, it was coming from someone who makes a living in the entertainment industry. My work would be both informed and heartfelt.

During the tour I had three more proctor sites booked in three new states. The first was at Laramie County Community College, in the southern Wyoming town where much of my singer's (Rob) family resides. This time, my math test was not only available as soon as I arrived, but the exam itself was also free.

A week later, we found ourselves with two days off in the beautiful town of Missoula, Montana. I took advantage of my free time on the first day to study a bit more for my accounting exam. On the second day, I ventured out on a 30-minute stroll down to the University of Montana campus. It offered a pleasant way to mentally prepare for my exam, as I anticipated a somewhat more intimidating environment this time around. The testing center was at a four-year university, and I wasn't quite used to the setting. For whatever reason, I associated more prominent educational institutions with additional red tape. This was not at all the case. The testing center was equitable to the colleges I had been visiting, although the campus itself was much larger and more majestic.

After two weeks venturing down the coast, we made it to Odessa, Josh's (my guitarist) and Rob's stomping ground in western Texas. We were invited to stay with Josh's parents, who are perpetually gracious hosts. Just down the street from Josh's parents is Odessa College, my third campus to visit during the DTB tour. The campus map was a bit convoluted, but I eventually found the testing center and completed my third algebra test for the semester.

A few weeks later I was back in the CSCC testing center to take my finals for each class and thought, "This is testing my patience." In fact, I was in a good mood, and my internal wisecrack forced a chuckle as I entered the exam room. I was greeted with silent, fleeting glances and frowning faces of the agonizing students preparing to commence with their own academic duties. Due to a mixture of my study habits, the excellent instruction of my algebra professor, Dr. Mingzhi Xu, and Matty's invaluable insights, I managed to earn an A+ on the algebra final.

Another Semester, Another Tour

Because we always seem to have a great time on tour with Downtown Brown, we booked another run with them in August, this time from the Midwest all the way up to Bangor, Maine. We hadn't been up there since the previous year when we played a little town the locals call "Bah Habaah." During sound check, the sound guy asked for "guitaaah," and then "bass guitaaah." When he got to me, he asked for "snaaah."

A few months earlier I had met with Jack Popovich[6], the Program Coordinator for the Finance program at CSCC. I had begun to consider the possibility of completing a finance degree. His advice was to enroll in the Corporate Finance course with Jill Cadotte[7]. "You will know very quickly whether or not you wish you continue on in finance." Accordingly, I did just that, along with taking PC Applications and Principles of Microeconomics.

The PC class offered several Word and Excel tricks that I still use to this day. Beyond that, it was primarily an easy three credits. On the contrary, the econ class effectively changed my entire outlook of the world. For instance, I was introduced to the concept of price elasticity of demand. Think of it as a balance between raising or lowering prices, and how much revenue you can bring in due to the response of customers. When prices are said to be inelastic, it means that raising prices will result in an increase in revenue.

Alternatively, when prices are elastic, raising prices will *reduce* your revenue. I always thought of it like an elastic band; elastic prices resist being stretched upward. When you attend a big festival show in which all the t-shirts are $50 and you buy one anyway, this indicates that the price is inelastic. Go to a small club show and you will quickly learn how elastic t-shirt prices are in that environment.

It becomes especially interesting to me when a band sells a shirt with only one color printed on it. It probably costs the group just a few dollars per unit (additional colors = higher

---

[6] He is now Dr. Jack Popovich as of 2018.
[7] Similar to Dr. Popovich, she is now Dr. Jill Cadotte as of 2018.

cost), so the inelastic nature of excited festival attendees is fascinating. I struggle with the idea of shelling out $50 for a one-color shirt, but I greatly admire the boundless dedication of touring merch store patrons.

Psychostick looking ultra-sad with Downtown Brown. From left to right: Bobbinz, Ron, Matty, Neil, Tony, me, Rob, and Josh.

Another invaluable lesson I learned was the concept of economies of scale. This one is a bit more intuitive. The more you buy or manufacture of a single product, the lower the individual cost of a given unit will be. When a band orders 100 CDs to sell, it might cost the group $5/piece. Order 1,000 and it might drop to $2/piece. This is also a good reason to become a Costco[8] member. It might cost an annual fee to sign up, but then you are offered far better deals in the long run by ordering products in bulk. Just try to resist buying milk in bulk if you don't have twelve kids.

My favorite class this term, however, was Corporate Finance, with the remarkable Jill Cadotte. She taught me all about things like the weighted average cost of capital (WACC) and the capital asset pricing model (CAPM). After one exam in which I couldn't quite figure out how to calculate some of the material, she invited me to her office on campus. We went through each question and she explained the how and why of each concept I didn't quite comprehend.

On another occasion, she offered her time on a phone call in which I fired off countless finance questions, and she brilliantly explained it all to me with more patience than I would have expected. Jack was absolutely right. Not long after that phone call, I committed to finishing my Associate's in Finance degree. Fortunately, the rest of my studies that semester didn't overlap with the tour except for the final two weeks of the term. To mitigate the entire issue, I booked my finals for the day before the tour even began.

Hard Lessons

Despite how it may appear on your social media feed, no one has a life of all wins. The same is true for bands. Over the summer we played the Rockstar Mayhem Festival in Maryland Heights, Missouri, a suburb of St. Louis. The headliner was Slipknot, and we were thrilled to see our friend Craig stop by the side of the stage to say hello as we were setting up. Of course, we were performing in the early afternoon, many hours

---

[8] Full disclosure: I own shares of stock in Costco, so I appreciate the patronage.

before Slipknot, so he had time to watch our 25-minute set.

The thing is, the way you finalize an experience is one of the most important parts of the whole ordeal. This is known as the peak-end rule[9], and it describes how the most intense point (the peak) and the finale (the end) are the most salient parts of an experience that we tend to remember best.

Hard Lesson #1:
Never put your flagship song last on the setlist.

As we prepared to triumphantly finish our 25-minute set, Josh noted that we were about 23 minutes in. Perfect. We started our song, Beer (which is two minutes long), when suddenly we heard the dreaded "you're done" from the sound guy and saw the "cut it" motion from the stage manager. I've seen it happen before, but it had never happened to us, certainly not in front of thousands of people. My stomach felt like I swallowed a rock the size of a tennis ball, but I instantly understood—we royally screwed up.

It wasn't the stage crew being mean or anything like that. We had worked with them in prior years on the same tour. We simply made the horrible decision to put Beer last on the setlist, not anticipating that the stage manager would cut us when we had two minutes left for a two-minute song. But his entire job is to keep the show on time. It would be entirely unprofessional to allow one band after another to play past the posted set times as they creep further and further behind until Slipknot gets cut short due to a curfew. As you can imagine, there is no way the production crew would allow that. St. Louis, we'll find a way to make it up to you.

Later that year, I was enrolled in three new classes:

---

[9] Yet another idea from Daniel Kahneman, eminent psychologist and Nobel Laureate.

Management, Business Language, and Principles of Macroeconomics. The macro econ course was by far the most influential on me as it was the impetus of my current worldview. I now recognize that we have a world economy with countless interrelated components, rather than independent domestic economies that only marginally interact. The imaginary lines we call borders seem increasingly silly as I progress in life.

That September, we embarked on a tour with Black Light Burns, with Wes Borland of Limp Bizkit fame fronting the band. I must say, I was pleasantly surprised to learn how friendly and reasonable he is despite his other band's massive popularity. That said, just because your tour mates are nice to you should not indicate that it is acceptable to be unprofessional.

Hard Lesson #2:
Not headlining? Get out of the way.

After a particularly enjoyable show in Austin, my camp was dragging a bit and we were slow to pack up. Downtown Austin is a notoriously challenging place to park, especially when you have a trailer in tow.

Accordingly, we opted to wait until things calmed down a bit outside and there was more space to load out. By the time we finally started packing up the trailer, Black Light Burns was also ready, and we were directly in their way. It is critical to understand that the TM did not simply throw a fit unjustifiably. The headlining band must be the first one in the club to sound check and the last one out after playing. If you waste time, it eats directly into your allotted time to sleep, which is a scarce commodity on tour. Accordingly, I took the brunt of the TM's anger at our unprofessionalism. Once again, we screwed up.

But again, we learned a valuable lesson.

Two days after the finale of the tour, we were flown out to play in Calgary, Alberta, which was our very first show outside of the United States. We were booked to play Noctis V Metal Fest, along with some of the most aggressive bands in the business. Some of the delightfully contentious groups included Pig Destroyer, Nunslaughter, Black Witchery, and one of the innovators of black metal, Venom.

After being picked up at the Calgary International Airport, we were escorted to the promoter's friend's house as a welcome to Canada. Evidently, it was Tea's (pronounced "tay-uh") tradition to bring the bands over to mingle, enjoy some drinks and snacks, and then depart whenever the need for sleep eventually came. It was the consummate social gathering put on by some of the nicest people I had ever met.

At one point, I ventured out onto the balcony to take a break from the commotion. Another band member was already out there, and my guess was that he was from England judging by his accent. I said hello and asked him about his band. He flatly replied, "Oh, I'm in Venom," with a look on his face reminiscent of a plea for mercy. I was never especially deep into the black metal scene, so I only knew of Venom by their reputation, rather than as a fan. I perceived it as an opportunity to ease his fears and casually replied, "Okay, cool," then promptly changed the subject. I could see the anxiety evaporate from his face as he realized he did not have to answer a thousand frantic questions about his popular band.

Hard Lesson #3:
Avoid liquors you have trouble pronouncing.

Later that evening back inside, our host was offering everyone a clear liquid she called "Slivovitz." I probably made her pronounce it several times before successfully parroting its pronunciation. To drink it is overwhelming, to say the least. That was the expiration of my composed sobriety.

The following morning, I looked up in horror to see a bottle of Crown Royal sitting on the hotel room desk. My heart sank into the bed as I recognized my fatal mistake. Did I really steal from the most generous host in history? I felt a level of shame unmatched by anything I had ever experienced. As I collected my thoughts, I began contemplating how exactly I would confess to my incredible transgression. A few hours later I finally found her and began to apologize profusely when she interrupted me. "No, I *gave* it to you. You didn't steal anything!" Words cannot describe my relief. Never again, Slivovitz.

By Halloween, we had developed a themed show for our comeback performance at Pop's in the St. Louis area. Dressed in Star Trek – The Next Generation uniforms, we marched onto the stage and announced that we would now finish our Mayhem set from July. As we began playing Beer as our opening song, half the crowd roared with laughter and the other half seemed confused but cheered with them. An hour and a full set later, we reached our final song as the headlining band that evening and began playing Beer for the second time. Again, half the crowd was stunned with mouths agape before cheering even louder than the first time we played the song that evening. We had finally redeemed ourselves.

CHAPTER 2013

 I know I'm in a comedy band, but this had to be a joke. Denver was contending with something called a "blizzicane," but I suspect the locals would still take it seriously without the theatrics. Originally a desert kid[1], it sounded apocalyptic to me. The Mile-High City, as only tourists seem to call it, was prepping for a massive blizzard while I was seemingly the only person trying to get *into* Denver.

The goal was to take my third International Finance exam at the Community College of Denver (CCD) before the city shut down. This time, the testing center charged a proctor fee of $35 for 2 hours, and this was the most challenging class I had taken to date, taught by none other than Jack Popovich. On top of all of that, I had piled up classes like a Colorado snowstorm. Along with International Finance, I had also

---

[1] The first two decades of my life were in the Phoenix area in AZ, so I didn't experience snow until second grade. It lasted for five minutes.

enrolled in Marketing Principles, Introduction to Psychology, and Legal Environment of Business.

As luck would have it, our friend Laura (who lets us stay whenever we travel through), had a friend willing to drive me to CCD before the storm shut the whole city down. It was that or nothing, as borrowing the van to try my luck that morning seemed increasingly reckless. I hitched a ride with Laura's friend Greg in his formidable truck, and we ventured out into the snow.

Evidently, while I was in the testing center, Greg's boss called and informed him that they had decided to close up shop. At least I wasn't making him late for work. Although this was the most challenging exam from the hardest class yet amid a flurry of difficult circumstances, I ended up getting 100%.

While the finance, psychology, and legal classes all lasted the duration of the semester, Marketing Principles was condensed into eight weeks. During that time, I had the pleasure of attending the National Association of Music Merchants (NAMM) show in Los Angeles. In fact, I was invited out by my friend Jesse "Turff" McInturff, who would later become my Debtors bandmate as well.

My mission was two-fold: to meet my long-time artist reps from Zildjian and Evans[2], and to get the inside scoop from Carvin Guitars. Strangely enough, one of the marketing assignments involved Carvin and its product line. I was at the only trade show in the world that could offer this type of front-line information on the products for the new year. I would have loved to see the reaction of my professor upon eyeing the 2014 innovations not yet announced in a 2013 undergrad paper.

---

[2]My Zildjian endorsement began in 2007, and Evans in 2010 when Psychostick was given a D'Addario factory tour.

Ready to make a good impression with Turff (left).

Leading up to our rendezvous with Polkadot Cadaver were several concerts in Florida. We had Orlando, Jacksonville, and St. Petersburg all booked consecutively, with St. Pete as our first show with Polkadot. As usual, I had exams for the psych and legal classes and found a suitable testing site at the University of Central Florida (UCF) in Orlando. Since it is a short drive from there to Jacksonville, I scheduled the exams at the UCF testing center for that morning.

The campus was enormous, and I found myself a bit unprepared for how much aimless walking there would be from the visitor's parking lot to the testing site. Ultimately, it only took me a few minutes to find it, and the campus was just down the road from where we were staying. It was a good lesson, regardless. If you want to remain on schedule, examine a campus map *before* arriving.

Polkadot Cadaver and Psych 101

Mercifully, the marketing class only overlapped with the

Polkadot Cadaver tour by three days. Now I was down to "only" three courses. This semester was the one and only time I attempted to juggle four classes simultaneously. Fortunately, I was successful with the undertaking, although it probably took a year or two off my life.

The legal class was also very challenging, but for a different reason. While I prefer to be a conceptual learner, it was *all* details. It makes sense, however, that it is not necessary to comprehend the reasons why a law has been implemented for one to understand the law itself. The important part is to recognize what a law means for an individual. It was also challenging to schedule and complete the 15 exams for the class, although only every third was required to be taken on campus.

In any case, my favorite course this semester was Introduction to Psychology. I did not know it at the time, but it incited a fascination with the brain that I would later embrace as a second, supplementary career. At the time, I was simply enamored with the material taught by Dr. Mark Polifroni[3]. One of the most interesting concepts I learned about was a condition known as blindsight. It concerns patients who are consciously blind in one or both eyes, yet they can visually detect objects subconsciously and avoid walking into them without knowing why. The idea is that the eyes are perfectly functional, but there is a disconnect in the brain somewhere in the occipital lobe such as the visual cortex, or in some cases, the optic nerve. There are several compelling theories as to why this happens, but I suspect they are all somewhat correct for at least some patients.

---

[3] Years later, I would visit him on the Ohio State University campus to thank him. Fun fact: Many university professors teach the same courses at community colleges for a fraction of the cost to students.

Meanwhile, the Polkadot tour was zooming right along. We had quickly befriended this lovely group of people and agreed to join them on another run the following year, but this time with their other band, Dog Fashion Disco (DFD). My best friend and our long-time tech and merch guy, Tony Schiavo, had developed a strong bond with them as well. He would soon join their camp as an indispensable touring member, which made me quite proud of him. Privately I was a bit melancholy that I would not see him as much in the coming years.

In any case, I was becoming increasingly busy as I muscled through the CSCC Finance program. I had been offered a membership with the Phi Theta Kappa Honor Society, along with a couple of other groups and started looking into the legitimacy of each. Notably, Phi Theta Kappa is an international society that is over 100 years old and strives to bring educational and scholarship opportunities to well-performing students of two-year colleges.

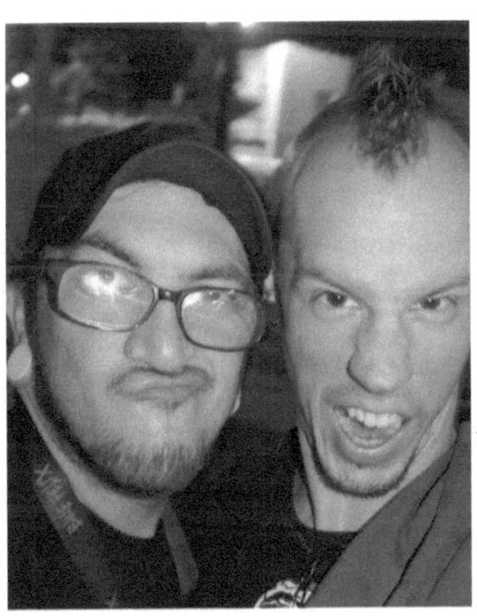

Looking fierce with the one and only, Tony Schiavo (left).

As luck would have it, my one-time $60 fee to join paid for itself many times over by that summer, as I had secured a $1,000 scholarship funded by GetEducated.com. Around the time I was awarded the scholarship, I was interviewed by a journalist from the site, Rachel Wang, for an article about my bizarre collegiate pursuits. I have participated in countless interviews with radio hosts, music journalists, and the like, but never had I been asked about how I manage to concentrate on assignments in a bumpy van. By the end of the semester, Psychostick had performed 185 shows since I began taking classes, a full 31% of the total days since the Autumn semester began back in 2011. It would turn out to be a rather unique article about a scholarship recipient.

Sleep Debt

During my preceding trip to LA for the NAMM show with Turff, we had agreed to try to find time to meet to write some absurdly aggressive songs for a band we would later name Debtors. The band name came to us on my visit to Minneapolis in which we began experimenting with various song ideas. The name originated from a concept I had learned in my psych class known as sleep debt. Cumulative sleep deprivation acts like the building mass of water behind a fractured dam about to break. It seemed appropriate considering the schedule we chose to keep for those few days. Fortunately, I had the foresight to work ahead on my schoolwork by a week so we could focus on composing songs without distractions.

I had a new round of classes by that summer, back to just three this time: Money and Banking, Business Applications, and Elementary Statistics. It was fascinating to learn the ins and outs of the banking system and how it operates in tandem with the Federal Reserve to balance interest and inflation. Business Applications was similar to the PC Applications class I had previously taken last summer, so it was fairly straight forward.

Interestingly, my favorite course was probably statistics. It was quite revealing to learn about probabilities in everyday life and how researchers come up with the numbers we so often hear about but are rarely explained. One fun example is the commonly used marketing ploy on toothpaste tubes. Have you ever noticed the phrase, "9 out of 10 dentists recommend [toothpaste brand]"? Well, sure. What they neglect to point out is that these dentists may select more than one brand to recommend. The doc just wants you to brush your teeth, not use a specific brand.

I also found a proctor site to visit that June while on Long Island, New York. To take my second Money and Banking exam, I found Nassau Community College[4] (NCC), not far from where Matty's parents were cordially housing us. Upon my arrival I learned that the testing center was adjacent to the Cradle of Aviation Museum, which features an LM-13 Lunar Module (which was supposed to be used on the Apollo 19 mission scheduled for the Copernicus Crater in 1973).

Evidently, some people thought that just 6 landings with a grand total of 12 humans to set foot on the Moon was sufficient to learn everything we needed to know about the Universe. I suppose the development of technology from Apollo used in MRIs, CAT scans, cordless power tools, dialysis machines, pacemakers, firefighter suits, solar panels, seismic activity detectors, burglar alarms, cooling suits for people born without sweat glands, and the Dustbuster is not enough to

---

[4] I'm now up to eight states for proctor sites: Colorado, Florida, Illinois, Missouri, Montana, New York, Texas, and Wyoming.

justify the cost of space travel.

In any case, the NCC testing center also charges by the hour, a custom I was growing to resent. I don't mind paying for the service, but in my opinion, it is a conflict of interest to pressure students further with a monetary incentive to finish quickly rather than focus on academic performance. Regardless, I completed my assignment and headed back to enjoy an exceptional meal with the family.

Crushing Candy 101

"Crushing candy?" Does that mean what I think it means? The day I met Justin Fowler from American Head Charge (AHC), he gleefully told me about his fondness for this "candy," which I took to indicate cocaine at the time. The 1995 Primus song, Wynona's Big Brown Beaver included the line, "candied up his nose," which immediately came to mind. I sighed internally, fully anticipating a depressing glimpse into the world of a severe drug addict on tour for the next month. I was thrilled to later realize that Candy Crush Saga is just a free video game available on mobile phones for players to…crush candy? I am still oblivious to the details of the game, but Justin quickly became one of my favorite humans I had ever met. He was just hooked on digital candy, not white powder.

As we pressed on as direct support for AHC for the next month, my last semester of the year included Intermediate Algebra, Business Ethics, and Introduction to Philosophy. The philosophy class was particularly enjoyable because of our marvelous instructor, Miriam Abbott[5]. On one occasion I sent her an email with a question regarding some supremely convoluted statement made by René Descartes. Her response

---

[5] Feel free to enjoy her 2013 TED Talk, Words with Math.

was, "I love, love, LOVE these kinds of questions!" This experience offered a drastic contrast between merely instructing a course and passionately teaching a class of students.

The most memorable assignment of the course was the Socrates Project, in which we were each tasked with researching a chosen philosophical question. My paper's introduction included:

> I like a challenge, so I posed a challenging query. *Is the meaning of life subjective to the individual or consistent among all living creatures?* This question has one inherent flaw. Rather than embracing the Cartesian approach, I made the assumption that we can actually find meaning in life.

I then interviewed a diverse group of 10 of my friends to get to the bottom of this meaning of life business. Can you predict the conclusion? First, my friends are an insightful bunch. I received 10 unique answers, each of which was thoughtful and compelling. I closed the paper by stating, "Perhaps I can find value in considering all of these divergent perspectives, rather than settling on any one of them."

The Business Ethics class also offered an interesting discussion on corporate social responsibility, taught by Dr. Bethany Poore. We were assigned hypothetical situations and tasked with determining the most moral policy for the company. It was a perfect counterpart to the philosophy class as many of the ideas applied to both. We also compared perspectives from economists, business owners, lawmakers, and so on.

For one assignment, I read the debate between Whole Foods co-CEO, John Mackey, and Nobel Laureate and

University of Chicago economist, Milton Friedman. While reading, I discovered the distinction between stakeholders and shareholders. Friedman argued that the only relevant concern for a company is to produce profits for its shareholders (the people who own shares of stock). Ever respectful but strongly opposed to the idea was Mackey, who contended that all relevant stakeholders are important, including customers, employees, suppliers, and even the community.

Frankly, the world just seems brighter if we consider others when making far-reaching decisions. Not long after, I read Mackey's book, Conscious Capitalism, further cementing the idea. Not only is it possible to be successful while also recognizing the well-being of others, but there is also a financial incentive to operate in that way. We all accomplish more by working together rather than divisively cutting each other down.

Intermediate Algebra was the most challenging course of the semester, but I once again had Matty in my corner to assist. As a 5-credit course, the workload was about equal to the other two classes combined. We studied factoring, quadratic formulas, imaginary numbers, you name it. I would have been proud of a solid B in the class, but somehow managed to earn an A. As we wrapped up the year, we enjoyed our victorious return to Trees, the botanical venue in Dallas. This time I did not harass anyone about phantom tour dates.

CHAPTER 2014

 *Buh-dum…buh-dum, buh-dum.* It was inescapable. *Buh-dum…buh-dum, buh-dum.* Is this really what the kids like these days? Yet another indistinguishable band was thumping away while wearing skinny jeans and perpendicular mullets. Confusingly, the band members (minus the drummer) seemed to believe they were crustaceans as they continually crab-walked around the stage. *Buh-dum, buh-dum.* Then some of them started jogging in place. It was perplexing. I want my metal to scare me, not perform calisthenics.

Of the 50+ bands to perform that day, we were absolutely the least cool group in attendance. That's nothing new. Later that day as we prepared to take the stage, the rain had begun pouring down. Just minutes into our set, a tidal wave came flooding onto the stage and the production manager threw in the towel. He rapidly cut the power to prevent a lightning storm from electrifying the equipment (and us) on stage. Better to keep it up in the clouds. One good thing came of the experience, however. It inspired the song, So Heavy, to be written for our upcoming album, Revenge of the Vengeance.

Revenge of the Capstone

Composing an album is kind of like taking a capstone course to finish a degree. At the time I was involved in both. We were writing a new album, but I was also enrolled in two simultaneous capstone classes. I anticipated the Finance Capstone, but it turned out that as a distance learning student my options were somewhat limited regarding the remaining Finance program requirements. Usually students also enroll in Finance Practicum/Seminar, but it was not available online, so I was allowed to substitute it with the Business Management equivalent, Case Study Strategic Management. For those keeping track at home, I was enrolled in Case Study Strategic Management, Finance Capstone, as well as Stars and Galaxies as my science elective.

The management capstone was taught by Dr. Bethany Poore, who I would later learn also teaches at Franklin University. I enjoyed her teaching style in the Business Ethics class so much I thought I'd join her once again. There was a heavy focus on research papers, which is my favorite part of being in college. I was assigned to research the management and business structure of several companies, some of which I admired, others not so much.

Notably, I studied McDonald's, Ford, and Southwest (the finest airline around). At the time of this project, Southwest was the only airline I researched that was even making a profit, not to mention expanding as a company. As Warren Buffett pointed out in his 1996 Berkshire Hathaway annual report, Virgin Group owner Richard Branson once explained how to become a millionaire. "There's really nothing to it. Start as a billionaire and then buy an airline."

Of a list of 20 companies available to research for my final project, I chose to take on the pharmaceutical firm, Bristol-Myers Squibb. As a biotech company, I thought it might offer me an interesting challenge as I knew very little about that sector at the time. I was quite interested to learn that the firm's pharmaceutical arsenal included several cancer-fighting drugs, a large HIV treatment division, and several other types of drugs for conditions such as Type 2 diabetes and other cardiovascular issues.

Meanwhile, the finance capstone incorporated the cumulative knowledge from all the courses to date. The major projects hit on personal finance, investments, corporate finance, and banking. The banking paper was the most compelling project for me because I was eager to research the catastrophic financial crisis of 2008 in conjunction with the Great Recession, from 2007-2009. The cause of the whole debacle is extremely complex. In short, it was ignited in part by deregulation, the subsequent housing bubble, and derivatives[1]. For context, Warren Buffett referred to derivatives as "financial weapons of mass destruction" in the Berkshire Hathaway 2002 annual report.

Jack Popovich, my Finance Capstone professor (also from the International Finance course), responded to my paper stating that he mostly agreed with my assessment, although I skipped over a few details that are not widely known. This piqued my interest, and upon my request he sent me a paper on deregulation that was too advanced for me to fully

---

[1] For a fascinating exploration of this fiasco, I recommend reading Michael Lewis's 2010 book, The Big Short: Inside the Doomsday Machine, later turned in a movie in 2015.

comprehend at the time. I appreciate that he did not try to shield me from taking on challenging subjects. That is how we advance.

Stars and Galaxies, however, was the most intellectually demanding course of the semester. As astronomy was my first scientific love, it was a genuine treat[2]. Dr. Anjali Gupta was the professor, but she is also a particle physics researcher who studies galactic nuclei and x-ray astronomy. She set a high bar, but I was quite proud to earn a B on the midterm as well as on the final. In the end, I somehow managed to squeak out an A in the class.

Back on Earth, we were still writing and recording the new Psychostick album, which would become Revenge of the Vengeance. The two songs I had the biggest hand in composing included Bruce Campbell and Quack Kills, a song about the most frightening beast of all, the duck. Naturally, I had a plan. In my mind's eye, I was certain that most people would assume that Rob, our singer, wrote the song and would likely pester him about it. "Are you really afraid of ducks?" "Were you bitten as a kid?" Six months after the album release, I finally let him in on my little scheme. It was a long con. To this day he regularly has fans inquire about the origin of his crushing duck phobia. To be fair, Rob does not actually fear ducks, as far as I know.

The day I completed my astronomy final was also the day I was named an All-Ohio Academic Team member (First Team) by the Phi Theta Kappa Honor Society and the Ohio Association of Community Colleges. It's a lot to rattle off, which makes it more prestigious. To accept the accolades, as

---

[2] I credit Stephen Hawking and his 2001 book, The Universe in a Nutshell for igniting my love of science. I have read each of his published books at least once and find it all tremendously inspiring.

well as a scholarship to help further my education, I attended a particularly fancy luncheon. It was attended by representatives and student award recipients from each community college in Ohio, and it was organized by table. CSCC was located closest to the buffet trays, which was fine by me.

I found myself sitting at a circular table seating about seven other people. I didn't recognize a single face, probably because I had never taken any traditional, on-campus classes. Everyone else seemed to know the gentleman next to me, however. As soon as he took his seat, the conversation abruptly transformed into a formal reception. It was an odd experience, as I am rarely in a situation that warrants this sort of behavior. Perhaps I just like to stir the pot, but I wanted to make the discussion a bit livelier. After this mysterious, clearly important person greeted the others at the table, he finally got to me. Rather than conceal my full identity and feel like a collegiate interloper, I opted to simply be myself. I introduced myself as the drummer of Psychostick and briefly explained what a "Psychostick" is, and then made a playful slight directed at one of the other tables. It was all in jest, as the mystery man obviously recognized.

A subtle smirk grew on his face as he rotated toward me to learn more about the strange newcomer to the academic banquet. As I was the only person at the table who did not seem to know him, he introduced himself. It was Dr. David Harrison, the President of Columbus State Community College. I should trash talk rival schools more often.

Summa Cum Laude

I would meet Dr. Harrison once again the following week as I crossed the stage to shake his hand and receive my diploma. I would love to recite his words of encouragement to me at that moment, but the 10 seconds of glory on stage as a new graduate is a little overwhelming. Alas, I have no idea what he said to me, but I do remember the tone of his voice. He remembered me from the week before and extended a warm and genuine message of congratulations. A moment later, I was urged on by the ceremony coordinators to make room for the remainder of hundreds of graduates that day.

While I am not fluent in Latin, I do know the words "Summa Cum Laude." Meaning, "with greatest praise," the words are included in the graduate program for the 2014 commencement ceremony that morning of Friday, May 9th. While the honors indicated my academic performance to date, it did not reveal the other preposterous details about my accomplishment. For starters, Summa Cum Laude describes a grade point average (GPA) of 3.950-4.000. Somehow, I managed to land on the extreme end of the scale.

Other absurd details include the fact that between my initial enrollment in September 2011 and my graduation in May 2014, I had performed 246 concerts in the U.S. and Canada. That means I had performed over a quarter of the days that elapsed from the first day of class to commencement. Additionally, I had proctored 39 exams in 8 states, not including the ones I took on campus at CSCC. I had completed 27 classes to finish my Associate's of Applied Science in Finance. What to do next?

A few months before graduating, I had investigated numerous educational institutions that could offer me an interesting new challenge. In my search I ended up speaking to a rep of a for-profit university which offered me the transfer of a whopping four classes into a bachelor's program. I think not. That experience made me lean toward a non-profit institution rather than a business.

It wasn't long before I had discovered Franklin University. It checked all the boxes. Accredited, non-profit, distance learning options, and another interesting new concept to me at the time. It caters toward working adults. Incredibly, CSCC and Franklin had teamed up to develop the Preferred Pathway program to make it easy for students to transfer. Franklin accepted a few more than four of my classes taken at CSCC. In fact, it transferred over the full 27.

Speaking with Dog Fashion Disco

I'm not sure what was trembling more, my voice or my hands. Why is it that I can perform in front of thousands of people without the jitters, but practicing a speech for my Oral Communication class in front of my friends had me quaking in anxiety? Fortunately, I picked a supportive bunch to help me rehearse my first speech for the course. It included members of Dog Fashion Disco (DFD), made up of several of the same people from Polkadot Cadaver. My audience also included Tony, who was now a part of the DFD camp. Still, I was uncontrollably nervous.

Naturally, the speeches became easier with practice. The first detailed my academic performance to date, which was weird. The official assignment was to film a one-take recording of my presentation in front of a small crowd of 4-6 people. Additionally, the camera had to show the back of their heads as I spoke. Fortunately, we were coming through Denver again, and once again staying with our friend Laura and her family. I convinced them to be my audience on the couch in their living room and recorded my speech. That had to be a bizarre experience for them.

From left to right: Rob, Matty, me, & Josh wearing his enviable Moon tie.

A couple of days before my speech in Denver, disaster struck. Our van was feeling under the weather and something had to be repaired. Don't ask me for details about this; I only know how to drive the thing, not fix it. We had to leave it at a shop in Omaha for several days to be repaired and opted to squeeze into a rental truck (the biggest vehicle available) and drive to Denver for our show. After the show, I spent the evening on the back patio with a bottle of Mountain Merlot and Elliot, our tech. We repeatedly listened to each of the songs on the setlist so he could learn the drum parts without actually playing them. The idea was for him to fill in on drums as I drove the truck back to Omaha to retrieve the van.

The rest of my camp would rent another vehicle and continue on to play Salt Lake City, Sacramento, and the Whiskey a Go-Go in Hollywood with Elliot as I drove back and forth across the country. The first stop was back in Denver to stay with Laura (again) and deliver my speech.

I drove over 2,900 kilometers in 5 days and slept at rest stops along the way. On day 4, I was determined to see the famous rock formations in southern Utah and drove a full 1,000 km before stopping. We reunited the following day in Las Vegas and I respectfully requested that someone take over to drive the rest of the way to the venue. Back on tour with my band and DFD, we played the Las Vegas Country Saloon that night, after which I slept particularly well.

During this debacle, I was taking two more CSCC classes despite graduating a few weeks before. This included Oral Communication and Introduction to Sociology in which I studied things like inequality, discrimination, and socioeconomic classes. I found sociology to be interesting but quickly learned that I was a bit more interested in individual quirks (psychology) than I was in societal issues. They are obviously both important, I was just developing a preference.

Additionally, I finally took my first Franklin class, Learning Perspectives. It was a valuable introduction to the procedures and requirements of my new school. I would need it to successfully double-major in Financial Planning and Financial Management in the coming years. Upon returning from the DFD tour, I still had three more speeches to compose, rehearse, and record while we were wrapping up Revenge of the Vengeance. One speech was on the history of space travel and technology. It was due the day after we finished the DFD tour, and we were threatened by the prospect of a tornado on the drive back. Luckily, Rob was at the helm and handled the violent air currents with grace and mastery.

There are two superheroes in our camp known to most as Murph and Kooks, or Patrick Murphy and Matt Kuchta, as they are identified by day. If you have ever seen a Psychostick music video, it was likely directed by Murph and starred in by Kooks. My plan was to ask Murph and Kooks to join me as audience members for the speech. But the wannabe tornado was at least vivacious enough to knock out the electricity in much of the Chicago area.

However, Murph and Kooks are two people who simply do not let you down. I had a speech to deliver to my instructor, and no matter what, they were going to make it happen. They somehow procured a portable generator for the lights and TV for my PowerPoint to go along with the presentation. They even filmed it for me. Naturally, its cinematography was much better than my previous speech in which I gaff taped a Zoom Q3 to a stand a started babbling.

The third was a persuasive speech advocating spaying and neutering pets. I pointed out that dogs can live an average of 1-2 years longer when spayed or neutered, while cats can live 3-4 years longer (depending on the size and average life span of the specific breed). This is partly because they are less inclined to wander around the neighborhood looking for dates and dodging cars. The final speech was about my childhood hero, Bruce Lee. He overcame innumerable obstacles throughout his life, and it seemed appropriate to tip my hat to him considering the summer I'd had.

The End of Proctors

I suppose a beachfront bar looking out upon the Atlantic Ocean just makes kids want to stage dive and do spin kicks. Not that there was even a stage at Sammy's Patio. Located a little northeast of Boston, Massachusetts, the crowd was so rowdy that some of the guys in the other touring bands came to our rescue.

As we performed, they held back the surge of flailing humans determined to crash into us. That is how we adopted our latest touring member, Rob "Manny" Whisenhunt. Once a police officer, Manny was then playing bass in Fungonewrong on our latest run along with DTB on the Revenge of the Vengeance tour. When his band later broke up, he joined our camp for more nutty tour adventures along with bands like Wild Throne, One-Eyed Doll, and Hed PE in the coming years.

I was also taking Global Issues as a condensed six-week course, which is a design that I would come to greatly appreciate. I don't enjoy tours that last for an entire season for the same reason I don't like classes that linger on for several months. I feel more motivated by classes (and tours) that are condensed into 3-6 weeks and don't overlap. The six-week course design of consecutive classes felt as though it was tailor-made with me in mind.

One part of the Global Issues course involved each student being assigned a different country to study during the term. I was given Romania, so my task was to write a paper all about the Romanian culture, political structure, economics, industries, famous locals, and so on. Part of the assignment was to contact someone from the country and conduct an interview. I eventually discovered Valentin Todorica, a native from nearby Moldova as an alternative to Romania. As the official language of both countries is Romanian (but known as Moldovan in Moldova), I was fortunate to learn that many people in the region also speak other languages such as Hungarian, Ukrainian, German, Russian, Turkish, French, and over a quarter of the population even speaks English.

I do not wish to ignite any heated discussions regarding regional politics, but the borders have changed numerous times over the years. Thus, the distinction between Romania and Moldova is somewhat a matter of perception. Additionally, the disputed territory of Trans-Dniestr (sometimes spelled Transnistria but known as the Pridnestrovien Moldavian Republic by the government) along the Ukrainian border is an ongoing issue and is considered a cultural open wound. It is currently recognized as a part of Moldova by the United Nations, but its own independent state by some.

I was also a bit horrified to learn that the ethnic group known as the Roma (or Romani) are widely scattered across the world and considered by some of the more dim-witted *Homo sapiens* to be lesser human beings. They are sometimes pejoratively called Gypsies, a term I had no idea was used in such a problematic way. This class granted me one of the most valuable learning experiences of my entire academic career. It helped me tremendously in my quest to become a more civil world citizen.

Once I wrapped up Global Issues, it was back to 12-week courses. This time, I took Intermediate Macroeconomics and Income Tax Planning. It was a significant step up in intensity. While the econ class was tough, it was easily my favorite course at Franklin so far. I wrote several papers of which I was particularly proud, including one on inflation and another on the short-run model of a large open economy. As I said, it was a step up.

The tax planning course was just as challenging, but around this time I learned something game-changing about Franklin. It offers online proctor services through ProctorU. To explain, ProctorU is a company that provides secure online proctoring services via the student's webcam. Rather than trade years of my life scheduling campus proctor exams, I could now do it anywhere I had an Internet connection. I tested it out for my income tax midterm in November and it worked beautifully.

First, I scheduled my midterm to be taken at a specific time, and I was assigned one of their testing specialists. Then the assignment instructions were sent to that person, which detailed whether or not I was allowed a pencil and paper, a calculator, notes, a textbook, and so on. I was instructed to obtain a small mirror ahead of time (which the student presents to the webcam once logged in), along with an ID to prove I am who I say I am. My first reaction was, "Why not just hold up my laptop to move to camera around to show the desk? Then it hit me. Post-it Notes.

The specialist examined the edges of my screen from the reflection in the mirror, as well as the workspace around me to ensure I did not have anything I was not supposed to have. Finally, once the specialist was satisfied, I begin the examination while I was observed through my webcam from afar. It seemed creepy at first, but it was a whole lot easier than scheduling physical proctor sites on tour.

CHAPTER 2015

 The goal was a bachelor's, but my mind was now on a graduate degree. I had kept in contact with Dr. Harrison, the President of CSCC, and he invited me to join him for a chat in this office on campus. I wished to ask for his advice about pursuing a master's at Franklin. He greeted me graciously upon entering and directed my attention toward a stack of papers on his desk arranged vertically. On top (or most forward) was a recent article I had sent him about my academic successes. It included one of my goals to help other musicians learn more about personal finance and generally improve the financial situation of my peers.

It was a stack of articles that inspired him. He briefly pulled my article up to reveal the last article that made the cut. I was greatly humbled to find that it was a recent press release from Elon Musk and his company Tesla regarding their recent adoption of a new open-source approach to patents. Car manufacturers were much too slow in progressing electric vehicle technology, so they made their patents available for all to use to advance humankind. Finding myself in such illustrious company was alarming. I struggled to find my words for a moment before mentioning my new ambition.

Savvy life coaches do not simply give advice to others. Accordingly, Dr. Harrison did not overtly offer his opinion about me enrolling in grad school. Instead, he asked questions. His queries seemed methodical as he gradually led me to discover that this is exactly what I wanted to do. I would soon apply to the Franklin University Master of Science program in Business Psychology. I just had some other tasks to tackle first, such as the rest of my bachelor's.

Downtown Brown & URIZEN

The one and only class I took on campus my entire college career was Advanced Financial Management. This was the first time I had entered a classroom since graduating high school in 2002. It was another condensed course, and the first few weeks were largely a review of the material I learned in Corporate Finance a few years back. It didn't take long to accelerate into the truly complex topics, however. It was called "Advanced" for a reason.

Interestingly, one student (who admittedly had his entire tuition paid for by his parents) kept asserting that social programs are inherently flawed because they discourage recipients from stepping up and earning their keep. I understand the sentiment, but the irony was overwhelming. With the exception of grants and scholarships, I personally covered my tuition (about half to date). I do not fault anyone for accepting parental funds to attend university, but maybe put a cork in it and listen to the professor who was once the

CFO of a $3 billion bank.

After completing the finance class, we were back on the road with Downtown Brown and URIZEN for the second leg of the Revenge of the Vengeance tour. Once again, we were playing the West Coast but eventually looped back around to Odessa, Texas. However, this time we would play in Midland at a 21+ bar called Blue Max. We had been performing a rather profane song all tour known as NSFW, but Josh's sweet and virtuous parents would attend the show that night. We were all curious to see if Josh would nix the song from the setlist.

With his parents directly to stage right (Josh's side), we performed the set in its entirety. Josh's mom sat and watched us perform the song with a smile on her face but conveyed her disapproval later that evening. He earned some serious street cred that night.

With Advanced Financial Management out of the way, I was now only enrolled in Insurance Planning and Retirement Planning. The insurance class was quite revealing because it offered a new financial perspective. Insurance products are not only used to mitigate or reduce liability. They can also be very useful as an investment asset in a family's financial portfolio.

Meanwhile, the Retirement Planning course featured an 800-page textbook. We learned all the detailed differences between pensions, profit-sharing plans, IRAs, qualified plans, and so on. To my benefit, the class was instructed by Mark Massen, a financial wizard who has a supremely keen eye for detail. He taught me much more than just issues related to retirement, including things like exact APA formatting and regional spelling differences. It is sometimes the subtleties that most others miss which really sets one apart as a writer.

I ended up joining Mark's financial firm as an independent agent for a time to expedite my goal of helping musicians with financial needs. With his invaluable assistance, I obtained my Life, Accident, and Health insurance license one day in Columbus. I flew from Chicago to Columbus on St. Patrick's Day and successfully completed the mandatory practice exam, then the background check, and passed the actual exam before flying back to Chicago 10 hours later. I learned a huge amount from Mark and credit him (along with his wife, Sharon—also a Franklin professor) for being a significant inspiration to pursue a master's.

Psychostick, DTB, & URIZEN. From left to right: Rob, Neil, Josh, Matty, Bomber, Tommy, Nolan, Der, Bobbinz, Angel, Manny, me, Joe, & Rustin at the Blue Max. Joe wrecked his skateboard earlier that day, and right after this photo was taken, Rustin launched him into the air to tumble once again.

I later obtained my Series 6 and Series 63 financial certifications to gain the ability to offer additional financial services to clients. My goal was to help my fellow musicians by teaching them the fundamentals. After a while, however, the environment of the firm was too rigid for my taste as the office manager kept insisting that I quit school *and* music to focus solely on making money in finance. After three years of his attempted mental conditioning, I'd had enough and quit to pursue my real interests. I wish him the best, but our personalities simply did not mesh. I desire more in life than just being wealthy.

My final two classes at CSCC were Human Biology and Ethics, which I took over the summer along with Estate Planning at Franklin. To qualify for Human Bio, I had been studying independently for a bio placement exam. I had not formally studied biology since I was a sophomore in high school back in 2000 (the year Psychostick formed). Naturally, I was concerned I would do poorly on the exam.

Failing the placement exam would require me to extend my undergrad career to fit in developmental bio courses to satisfy the science elective requirements. As it turned out, the exam closely mirrored what I had studied, and I felt fairly confident with my performance. The testing center immediately sent my results to the chairperson of the Biological and Physical Sciences department. I found it rather intimidating to see the same name displayed on some of the textbooks on the wall as the one on the desk in front of me. Evidently, my performance was adequate, and he allowed me to enroll in Human Biology. I could finally study brains, a topic that was quickly pilfering my collegiate interests.

Finance was what got me into college in the first place, but I was becoming increasingly fascinated by the nervous system. My bio instructor, Merideth Sellars, was a wonderful instructor who was eager to teach me anything I wished to learn. On one occasion, she guided me through the convoluted details of capillaries. On another, I had the awkward task of completing bio labs while traveling with Mark Massen for a financial seminar put on for young financial planners. The lab assignment concerned homeostasis, and it involved me pacing up and down a Marriott hallway to monitor my pulse. Then I was found running up and down the stairs with a thermometer to assess my temperature as I was exercising. The final component required a row of cups filled with water at various temperatures. I was to dip my fingers in each to compare relative temperature changes. Mark was extremely amused and noted that I was "playing with water." I am certain the desk clerk started applying for new jobs that day.

A few weeks later my band was in Dallas to play a gaming convention and I was setting up for my final lab assignment. This time I was instructed to tape my thumbs to the palms of my hands and complete several tasks to demonstrate our profound dependence on opposable thumbs. The whole ordeal was too much for my bandmates to restrain their jokes. To my dismay, Matty asked, "Are you *opposed* to this assignment?" Mercifully, everyone left the room for a moment, and I quickly took advantage of my newfound privacy to complete the final task. I then learned what it is like to bumble around like a quadruped.

Meanwhile, I was taking my second philosophy class, this time on Ethics. It was great fun because the course was structured a bit differently. Rather than teach the students somewhat individually, the whole point was to debate the big issues in society, such as religion, abortion, euthanasia, divorce, capital punishment, and animal rights.

Perhaps this warrants a discussion about my view of the world. From my perspective, religiously-motivated denial of evolution is akin to politically-motivated climate change denial.

Both fields boast an ever-expanding ocean of evidence, which keeps rising like the world's sea level. Believe whatever you want, but if someone spouts science denial to me in an educational setting, that person can expect an intellectual quarrel.

Everyone is entitled to an academic environment free of verbal abuse, but obtuse ideas are not immune from a rebuttal. For instance, consider anthropogenic global warming (human-caused climate change). Virtually every Ph.D. on the planet agrees on the science. In fact, the greater the person's expertise in the field, the higher the likelihood of that person agreeing with the scientific consensus. The only people who dispute the reality of climate change are those who are either scientifically illiterate or avid members of a political party whose leaders have a financial interest in keeping things just the way they are.

Perhaps I'm just a trouble-maker, but the first "debate" was so dull I do not even remember the topic. Accordingly, I decided to play devil's advocate for the remainder of the class. During a subsequent debate, I was bored with the state of everyone agreeing with one another that divorce is unacceptable because "they made a promise to each other, and to God." Thus, I decided to stir the pot. I carefully argued the merits of divorce in the case of a couple getting married before they reach age 25. This age is around the time the prefrontal cortex (which is associated with decision making) finishes developing. If "adults" are legally allowed to marry at age 18 without fully-functional brains, how can they be legally capable, in a contractual sense?

I did not make any friends in my Ethics class. Most of them seemed to believe that I despise children, which I found hilarious. During the next debate, they decided that I hate animals as well after I pointed out the ethical requirement to use animals for medical testing before a treatment can advance to human trials. Like it or not, every single legal vaccine and medicine you have ever taken was developed using animals as test subjects. If you enjoy not contracting polio or smallpox, you have animal trials to thank. Besides, researchers are strictly regulated and go to great lengths to minimize any needless suffering or harm to animals. It is just naïve to think that the modern human world would even be possible without animal testing.

In the final week, I kept coming across logical inconsistencies regarding students stating that they believe in the philosopher Thomas Aquinas and his Theory of Natural Law yet defending abortion or euthanasia. One cannot consistently claim to be in favor of Natural Law (in which everything in the Universe has meaning, which comes from God), and then say you believe in abortion or euthanasia. Even if you mean to defend women's rights or wish to minimize the pain of the dying, it simply doesn't hold up.

Thomas Aquinas further argued that religion is a prerequisite to morality. As a non-theist, I find this idea both pretentious and frankly, rather insulting. Accordingly, I trashed his entire premise without remorse. My professor (who has a Ph.D. in Theology), offered a single sentence as his comment on my paper. "You show better understanding of Aquinas than a lot of religious students." I might have irritated him to no end that semester, but I earned an A+ on that paper.

The most complex course this term was Estate Planning. It incorporated elements of personal finance, taxes, insurance, and retirement planning, and lumped them all into one comprehensive study of passing along assets to heirs. It was challenging, but I completed the final project in a hotel room in Clarksville, Tennessee before playing a show that night. I was to give my presentation at 7 that evening, then got picked up by Rob to head back to perform.

Final exams, on the other hand, were still to come. I scheduled all three for the term to be taken within 24 hours at different locations in Florida between shows. The first, my biology final, I took in the morning using ProctorU from a hotel room in Orlando. Thankfully, Rob made sure to vacate the room while I was taking my exam so I could concentrate and not confuse my testing specialist peering at me through the webcam.

Immediately after I finished, we drove to St. Petersburg for our show at the State Theater. I commandeered the upstairs green room to take my Ethics exam. Unfortunately, one of the local bands had decided to use it to smoke weed, so I had to boot them out, much to their dismay. To discourage any unnecessary distractions, I wore my new Bose QC15 noise-cancelling headphones and set up a paper sign next to my workspace that read, "Do not disturb—testing." Halfway through my final, someone tapped me on the shoulder, so I shooed the person away and pointed to the sign without looking up. I later learned that it was our well-intentioned tech, Manny, who had come to deliver me beer tickets. The following morning, I took my third (and last) final for Estate Planning, again with ProctorU. Upon completion, we were off to South Carolina.

Batting 1,000

Psychostick celebrated its 1,000[th] show in Birch Run, Michigan on August 8th at a music festival called Dirt Fest. The night before, we suffered yet another broken trailer incident during an all-nighter and arrived eight hours later than we hoped. However, the show itself was incredible. Upon playing our final note in front of thousands of attendees, the festival promoters presented us with a celebratory cake featuring spikes to emulate Rob's stage hat. Honestly, I only saw it for a fleeting moment because I had to remove my drums from the stage and out of the way. To whomever ate the impressive looking cake, I hope it was delicious.

I then hauled my drums to the adjacent stage because I had agreed to allow Lou from Kottonmouth Kings borrow my kit for their performance. Evidently, they had flown in without gear. I was fine with it because I have a soft spot in my heart for the group. They happen to be the first band I ever saw perform in 1999. After all that, we drove all night to cross the border for our first two Canadian shows we had ever played while touring in a van. First, we played in Toronto, then Hamilton. Fittingly the run was with Wolfborne, a band from Vancouver, BC.

Not long before our first tour in the United Kingdom, I learned of my acceptance into grad school. It was a wild concept to me. I would soon be enrolled to pursue my M.S. in Business Psychology, once again at Franklin University. To top it off, I was allowed to take advantage of the Joint Study program, which allowed my first graduate course to fulfill the last elective requirement for my bachelor's.

Dog Fashion Disco in the UK

Flying to London to embark on a UK tour with DFD while completing two simultaneous capstones is not something I would recommend to the faint of heart. However, I needed to complete the Financial Policy Seminar and the Financial Planning Seminar to fulfill the major requirements of my degree. The run was called the Ugly Americans Tour, and we had a splendid time performing for people with much more attractive accents than our own.

This was also the one and only time my band has toured in a bus. Known as a "nightliner" in the UK, we were fortunate enough to have an ever-snarky driver named John, who was impeccably English. The day we landed in London and reunited with DFD in customs, we exited the terminal to hunt down the nightliner and quickly found our new home for the next week and a half. John muttered, "What are you waiting for? Get the hell on board!"

I spent several late evenings in the passenger seat (left side) talking to John. He was a fascinating character. On one occasion I realized he was swerving across the lanes as the roads curved and he recognized my sudden discomfort. "Don't worry about that. It keeps the ride smoother so your mates can sleep." To be fair, it was always a very smooth ride as he weaved in an out of lanes, provided no other cars were around him on the road. I also learned that he owns a second home in Romania, and it probably surprised him that I was so excited about it. I explained the paper I wrote, which seemed to impress him somewhat. He had never been to the U.S. and had no intention of ever doing so, and I suppose he thought it was interesting that I prefer to be a world citizen more than a nation's citizen.

John also had the *best* stories. On one occasion, he was driving a crew nightliner for the rock band U2 around Europe and their singer, Bono, refused to drink anything but Fiji brand bottled water. John found that to be preposterous, so when the shipment was to arrive a day after they were set to depart for the second leg of the run, John spent the evening filling up each empty bottle with tap water. Bono never complained.

On another tour, he was driving an auxiliary nightliner for the pop singer, Lady Gaga. It was empty, save something in the pair of safes up at the front. One night at a border crossing between Hungary and Austria, he was stopped for an inspection and the officers demanded that he open each safe. He didn't have the keys, so he called Lady Gaga's manager back in London.

The manager took the first flight he could get on and flew in to meet John to get him back on the road. Keys in hand, the manager opened the first safe and pulled out an extravagant hat. When pressed by the border patrol about the meaning of this, he explained that it was Lady Gaga's $150,000 hat that she wishes to keep with her on tour, but not on her own bus. I can only imagine the befuddlement the guards felt as they asked him to open the second safe to learn that it was a second hat. This one was a $250,000 piece of headwear.

One day in Newcastle, John told me about how he met the metal singer, Marilyn Manson. According to John, Manson tries to push everyone to a breaking point just to see how much he can get away with. I suppose he is so famous by now that he's just bored. The day he met John, Manson instructed the entire caravan to stop so he could get a smoothie. The whole party stopped briefly, and I can only imagine how confusing that would have been for the person working behind the counter to see a parade of buses and only receive a single order for a smoothie.

After they departed, Manson reportedly threw a fit. He did not get the correct type of straw that he prefers for drinking smoothies. He demanded the tour turn around and backtrack an hour to retrieve the correct straw. Stopped briefly on the side of the road for the TM to explain this to each driver, John wasn't having it. He walked over to the lead nightliner and knocked on the door. "Mr. Manson?" He answered, smoothie in hand. "I am the driver for one of your nightliners and I'm carrying a lot of your equipment. If you are going to act like a child, I'm flying home. If I fly home, the tour is over because you don't have your equipment." After a moment to consider, the tour party carried on, and he did not retrieve his prized straw. Instead, Manson has insisted that John be his personal driver for every European tour since the day they met.

The UK nightliner Psychostick & DFD shared with John at the helm.

He once had the opportunity to drive Tim Robbins for a few days to attend a bluegrass concert, as the 6'5" actor was scheduled to perform there with his band. Upon meeting him but hardly looking up from his itinerary to view the man, John asked, "Mr. Robbins?" The actor glanced down at him and paused for a moment. "You don't know who I am?" John replied, "Of course I do. You're Mr. Robbins. Now let's go." The actor let out a hearty laugh and told him they would be good friends.

By the time I met John, he was then vaguely aware of some film Mr. Robbins had been in years ago but had never bothered to watch it. I couldn't believe it. "You drove Tim Robbins to his concert, but you haven't seen the Shawshank Redemption?" John shrugged. Knowing he had a DVD player on the nightliner, I later hunted down a used copy of the landmark film at a local video store for £1. When I gave it to John, he just laughed. "Look at that. It's Mr. Robbins. Maybe I'll watch it someday."

I enrolled in the Financial Policy Seminar to fulfill the last Financial Management requirement. It includes elements from the corporate side of the finance world, including investing, money and banking, multinational finance and all the other topics I studied at CSCC. It was a 15-week course that began on September 7th, which happened to be the same day we flew to the UK for two weeks. Naturally, I worked ahead and completed most of the coursework for those two weeks before I left the country. That was a good move, because I've never been so busy in my life as I was during that trip. For the first half of the term I did papers on things like CAPM, WACC, NPV, IRR, and TVOM. It was basically alphabet soup that represented financial principles and theories.

After completing possibly the most enjoyable tour of my career all over England and a bit of Scotland, we had three days off back in London. The idea was to enjoy a short vacation and see the city. However, after flying in to the UK and playing nine frenzied shows consecutively for people who had been waiting for us to come for potentially years, we were pooped.

A friend of ours in London offered to let us stay at her loft with her roommates. With the four band members, Murph and Manny, all the human roommates, and all their pets, there were 23 living beings in that home for those few days. I found a perch in the stairwell between a bathroom and the kitchen and worked on my papers. Finally, by our final evening in the UK, I logged into my class at 2 in the morning, British time.

Thankfully, it was just a normal class (not a presentation), so I did not need to talk much, which would probably have kept the roommates up. By 4 a.m. we loaded into a taxi to head back to Heathrow to return to the U.S.

During the second half of the term, I had the absolute pleasure of working on a team project with 12 students. I'm not typically fond of group projects, but this team was unusually fantastic. We boasted 2 finance majors, 4 HR, 5 marketing, and 1 eMarketing. By the end of the whole thing, our final (which was called a strategic plan, and it was for a fictitious coffee company) was a 320-page paper. It contained 14 pages of references, and by the end I referred to it as a dissertation.

Back in the U.S., the second leg of the Ugly Americans Tour with DFD was wrapping up. By the 23rd of October, it was now the end of my 31st trip around Sol. This time we were at the Foundry in Cleveland, Ohio, playing for a packed house. At one point I was evicted from my drum throne and instructed to let the rest of my band play a death metal rendition of the birthday song. With Rob behind my drums, I decided to enjoy the festivities from the crowd. I dove into the dense sea of humans as they slowly made room for my feet to touch the floor. I was surrounded by enormous fans all twice my size. Thus, I knew they could handle me being a little rowdy. As my band started into the birthday song, I began to push and initiated an official birthday mosh pit. The crowd gleefully joined in, and I was immediately squished.

Just after the tour wrapped up, I attended an induction ceremony for the Sigma Beta Delta International Honor Society for Business, Management, and Administration. It did not conflict with my Phi Theta Kappa membership, as this one was not intended for students of two-year programs. I was also finishing Financial Planning during that time. It encapsulated the one-on-one personal finance elements, rather than mathematical financial theory. It incorporated and combined the finance classes I had taken at Franklin. The final paper was a comprehensive financial plan for a fictitious family, and arguably more complex than the group coffee paper. This is what was happening in my life while I was composing the paper (due December 19):

December 9 - 90-minute team (coffee) presentation in Chicago

December 10 - Show in Milwaukee, WI

December 11 - Show in Ringle, WI

December 12 - Show in Minneapolis, MN

December 13 - Drive back to Chicago, IL

December 14 - "Oh Tannenbaum" video shoot

December 15 - Drum recording session

December 16 - Drive to Columbus, OH to be a board member[1]

December 17 - Drive to Dayton, OH for my Financial Planning final presentation, then appeared as a board member for another class

December 18 - Submitted Financial Planning final paper

December 19 - Enthusiastic slumber

Award Ceremonies

Upon accepting the 1902 Leadership Circle Scholarship[2], I had a lot of thanks to give. The scholarship is awarded annually,

---

[1] Dr. Sharon Massen's Business & Professional Writing students present to a "board" for finals. I was invited to be a board member on several occasions.

[2] A portion of this book's proceeds are earmarked for this fund. See copyright page for details.

and the recipient is gifted $4,000 for tuition. I had submitted an 832-word essay (with a 750-word limit) answering the question, "How do you represent the essence of Franklin University's namesake Benjamin Franklin?" The essay was a condensed version of the book you are reading now, but with some Benjamin Franklin quotes sprinkled in for good measure. I also included a flattering letter of recommendation from Mark, my professor who had witnessed me "playing with water" earlier that year.

Murph helped me film a video as a "thank you" meant to be shown at an upcoming Franklin University staff and faculty assembly. The script I wrote was genuine and heartfelt, but it seemed a little dry as we filmed it. Accordingly, I stacked up all my textbooks from recent classes as well as a few from my upcoming graduate courses and spoke about studying on tour. To emphasize my point, I performed a few quick repetitions of a drum rudiment called a "swiss army triplet." Later in the video (upon Murph's instruction), I paused to pick up a small log and placed it in the flaming fireplace, and then immediately continued speaking as if there was not just a bizarre fireplace interlude. I will forever wonder if the video was appreciated by the generous scholarship donors, or if it just confused those in attendance.

CHAPTER 2016

Make no mistake; I'm a nerd. But perhaps I am a nerd of a different sort than my friends. As we have already established, I don't know a thing about video games such as Candy Crush Saga. In fact, the only video games I have ever really played are Descent II and Descent III, probably because they remind me of the ships from Star Trek. Maybe it is because I enjoy science fiction novels and films so much. Some of my favorite movies are Aliens, Sunshine, and the Matrix. My favorite television show is the Battlestar Galactica reboot. One day I'll buy a Tesla and name her Caprica 6. I also do not suffer sitcoms, but I would reconsider if they took place on a space station.

Beyond films and television, I also read a great deal, but mostly nonfiction these days. However, one of the most mind-bending sci-fi novels I have ever encountered is Spin by Robert Charles Wilson, in which the Earth is suddenly surrounded by an apparent membrane that massively distorts how planetary inhabitants experience time. Another favorite is A Signal Shattered by Eric Nylund, about a crazy technology-trading alien bent on destroying humanity. I also enthusiastically blasted through Children of Time by Adrian Tchaikovsky, about a planet of sentient space spiders. I am thoroughly enjoying the sequel as I compose this very book.

I have finished about 35 books every 12 months for the past several years. I once decided that it is reasonable to read as much when there are 365 days in a year (ignoring leap years). If an average book length is, let's say, 10 chapters long, I could finish it in a week and a half if I read a chapter a day. That comes to 36.5 books a year, but let's call it 35 to account for days I don't have time to pick up a book due to a holiday or birthday engagements.

This is what made it so bizarre for me to attend MAGFest. Located at the illustrious Gaylord National Convention Center in National Harbor, Maryland, this "Music and Gaming Festival" boasted more than 20,000 eager attendees. I had been to the same convention center for a financial conference the previous month, and the contrast was staggering. It had transformed from a sea of suits to a crazed crowd of cosplay in just a few weeks. Many of the attendees looked forward to this event all year and they weren't going to waste time doing anything silly like sleeping.

It is challenging to describe just how strange it is to be at a multiple-day, 24-hour party when you are the sole person not in on the jokes. It simply isn't my world, although I admire the general level of devotion demonstrated by the attendees and staff. I can still recall one running joke that probably had something to do with a video game or TV character. One person would begin yelling, "Ohhhhhhhh" and seemingly everyone within earshot would quickly join in as the tone and volume would ascend dramatically. These kids are rowdier than some punk rock shows I have attended.

Rob meets his match on stage at MAGFest.

While I used to feel overwhelmed by crowded events such as this, I now view it as an opportunity to be a cultural anthropologist. I study the odd customs and languages spoken. Sometimes the subject is LARPing[1], and then perhaps obscure board games. Talk to me about the neuro-economical drift-diffusion model concerning decision making and I'll sound just as nerdy. One preference is not superior to another; they are just different.

Introduction to Logic and Critical Thinking Skills. That was the final undergrad class I needed to take before I could move on to graduate courses. Fortunately, each class was scheduled as a six-week course from here on out. Additionally, I had the

---

[1] Live Action Role Playing.

good fortune of once again having Miriam Abbott as my professor, who previously taught my Intro to Philosophy class in 2013. This time, we got to study the amusing world of logical fallacies. One assignment instructed us to hunt down interesting examples in the news or popular media. I proceeded to pick on the rapper and questionable authority on planetary physics, B.o.B. This person believes the world is a disc rather than an approximate sphere, and flatly states as much on his Twitter account. To me, the silliest part is that he posts comments and pictures about it and "tags" his location using his mobile phone.

As he is obviously unaware, the global positioning system (GPS) is accomplished using a network of telecommunication satellites orbiting at around 14,000 kilometers per hour. Each satellite contains an atomic clock accurate to a billionth of a second (a nanosecond), and your device on the ground compares the time on Earth to the time in orbit. However, without compensating with calculations from Special and General Relativity developed by Albert Einstein, the GPS satellites would become increasingly out of sync as their respective times drift apart. This is because the satellite is zooming around much quicker relative to us on the ground, and we experience more gravitational effects on the ground than the satellites do up in orbit. It's a less extreme version of what happened on the planet near the black hole in the movie Interstellar. Without accounting for Relativity (which requires a spherical Earth), GPS tech wouldn't work, and our rapper friend wouldn't be able to tag himself in his fallacious Twitter posts.

I also picked on the movie, Lucy, for its precisely false interpretation of neuroscience. Even the movie poster makes the erroneous claim, "The average person uses 10% of their brain capacity." Ignoring the grammar, this is still a comment worthy of head shaking and a call for ibuprofen. The brain is the most expensive real estate in the entire body. The human brain makes up a mere 2% of the total body mass yet gobbles up about a quarter of its energy. Why on Earth would the human brain evolve to utilize just 10% of its capacity? That would be like only 10% of the shops in Times Square bothering to open for business on Black Friday.

Nekrogoblikon

A little over a week into the Nekrogoblikon (Nekro) tour with URIZEN, we were struck with tragedy. Our great friend and tour mate, Rustin Luther from URIZEN, was feeling the effects of some optical issue by the time we reached Houston. One of his eyes was rotating inward, and none of us knew what to think of it. He wore an eye patch for a time but was soon hospitalized. I would later learn that he had developed a brain stem glioma, and the prognosis was grim. He was given about another year to live.

Rather than lament about the tragic early death of the shining Texas star, allow me to jump ahead a bit to reminisce about his visit to the Psychostick studio during the DO album recording sessions. Rustin was in town for a concert and stopped by to play an "extrovert villain" on our new song, Introvert Party Time. He skillfully recorded numerous perfect takes including, "HEY, you watch the sports ball game? He hit a touchdown and found a goal basket!" He was the best of us, and we miss him dearly.

Back in 2016, I was beginning my first grad school class called Introduction to Business Psychology with professor Diane Alexander. People often ask, "What exactly is business psychology?" To me, it is a business degree from the point of view of a human. Every customer you will ever have for your products and services will be human, unless of course aliens swing by to purchase some wares. Accordingly, thinking about business from a psychological perspective makes perfect sense. Master of Business Administration (MBA) degrees include courses on management, economics, human resources, marketing, and so on. Business Psychology does as well, but from a more human-oriented vantage point.

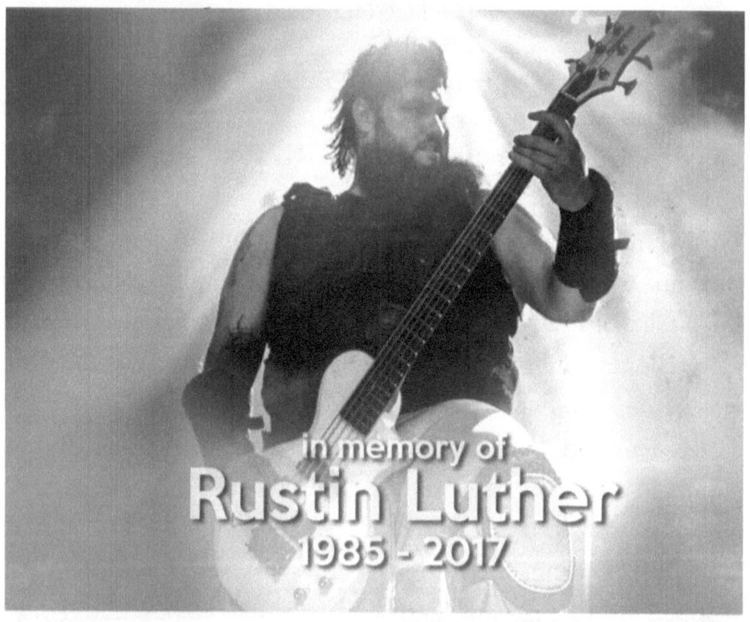

Rustin looking particularly metal. Taken from the DO album tray.

The program also has a heavy neuroscience component, which was perfectly aligned with my interests. Probably my favorite paper (and the most challenging) was on a chosen type of neuroimaging technology. We were given a list of neuro alphabet soup from which to choose. It included EEG, MRI, fMRI, CAT, PET, SPECT scans, and several more. Reading the overview, nothing was quite capturing my attention. I wanted to investigate non-invasive imagers, meaning scans that do not require injections of radioactive material like CAT, PET, & SPECT. However, I had already heard of EEG and MRI scanners. I needed a challenge. I wanted to study something I couldn't initially pronounce.

Upon consulting The Scientific American: Brave New Brain, a book by Judith Horstman, I discovered just what I was seeking. It was called magnetoencephalography (pronounced mag-nee-toh-en-sef-uh-log-ruh-fee), or MEG for short. I asked my professor if I could research that instead, and she gave me a green light.

MEG is non-invasive (no radioactive tracers), plus it detects brain activity directly, rather than by indirect methods, such as blood flow or glucose uptake. fMRI scans, as useful as they are, conduct indirect scans, so they detect the iron in the hemoglobin of the blood to determine where the brain is the most active. In contrast, MEG imagers monitor direct magnetic fields emitted by firing neurons. However, the magnetic fields are so weak the machine requires a shielded room and hundreds of small sensors with noise-cancelling software. Additionally, modern MEG machines require the use of liquid helium to cool them down to around -200 degrees Celsius. As you can imagine, they are expensive gadgets.

In case you are wondering, Nekro does, in fact, perform with a spooky goblin known as John Goblikon. One of my favorite memories with Mr. Goblikon is when we were backstage one evening and I said something inappropriate. "You're the worst, Alex." Being told by a goblin that you are "the worst" makes you reconsider the life choices that brought you to that moment.

Meanwhile, the seven-week Nekro tour was coming right

along. My band flew right through customs at the Canadian border, but several members of the tour party did not make it successfully. As I understand it, Canada has a strict no-DUI policy, so the tour members who had made bad choices previously in life were not allowed to perform with us in Montreal and Toronto. Yet another reason to avoid driving while you are impaired. However, it was quite impressive to see the bands perform even without the full crew and no practice beforehand. What beasts.

Next up was Individual and Organizational Psychology. One of the most interesting ideas from this class concerned biomimicry. This is essentially the practice of designing machines to emulate creatures found in nature. As an example, the wing of a plane might mimic the wings of a bird or the fins of a shark. Another example might be the design of a solar panel array after a sunflower's cluster of ray florets. I had no idea biomimicry is such a pervasive inspiration in modern engineering designs. However, it makes sense to model things after designs that evolution has been tinkering with for millennia.

After considering numerous options for how to complete my next final presentation, I asked Nolan McCormick of URIZEN fame if he would be interested in filling in for me on the night in question. Much like Elliot, Nolan was the hero of this tour, as he learned many of our songs and performed one per night leading up to the presentation.

When the day grew closer, the professor opted to cancel the formal presentation portion in favor of submitting extensive PowerPoints. Rather than perform the entire show with us when I couldn't, we opted to invite Nolan to continue drumming on one song a night for the duration of the tour. He usually opted to play So Heavy. His formidable double bass skills are enviable, to say the least.

Band members & crew from Psychostick, Nekrogoblikon, & URIZEN, including Rustin photoshopped in on the far-right side, and Daniel on the top left.

Summa Cum Laude Secundus

With two graduate courses under my belt, my undergrad commencement ceremony that May was admittedly a bit underwhelming. Besides, my bandmates were not able to attend this time to celebrate with me. In any case, I was awarded my diploma for a Bachelor of Science degree. Although I had double-majored in Financial Planning and Financial Management, my diploma did not reflect it. It included only the part about it being a bachelor's degree. However, it once again read, "Summa Cum Laude."

I was also amused to finally meet Dr. Bruce Campbell, the program chair of the Financial Management program. He is of no relation to the actor, Bruce Campbell, who we admiringly sang about on Revenge of the Vengeance in 2014. However, he is in good company with a fine name such as that. In any case, I had once again completed a degree with a 4.0 GPA, despite my increasingly bizarre collegiate circumstances.

Conventions & Festivals

As a fan of the aforementioned film, the Shawshank Redemption, it was a pleasure to explore the Ohio State Reformatory where the movie was filmed. However, numerous other people on the prison tour had brought along "ghost detector" applications installed on their "smart" phones to purportedly inform them of paranormal activity. I later learned that many of the apps are free to download, but offer various bonus features you may purchase. One charges $4.99 per week and offers "Real-Life Ghost Stories," whatever that means. It also features the disclaimer: "Given the fact that paranormal activity cannot be verified scientifically, we can't guarantee that the app communicates with real spirits." No way! It was all very confusing, but the prison tour itself was great. My band would later set up and perform in front of the prison as part of Ink the Clink, a festival in which you can watch rock bands or go inside and get a tattoo in a former prison.

We would later perform at Too Many Games in the Philadelphia area, a wonderful convention that we would later come to be the "house band" and headline each year. We also performed at Danville Comicon, another convention, but this time in Illinois. Then we returned to perform at Dirt Fest for the sixth consecutive time, where we had played our 1,000[th] show the year before. This year's lineup included one of my favorites, a disorderly band called Hatebreed.

The following month we were graced with the likes of Lords of the Trident to perform at yet another convention. It was called Geek.kon and was in the Madison, Wisconsin area. I believe this event was my introduction to LARPing as well. It included many fierce-looking goblins and elves. I bet John Goblikon would reign supreme on that battlefield.

Geek.kon was also the show in which the grumpy promoters decided they did not like our profane merch. We were selling foam fingers, not unlike the ones you might see at a sporting event signaling to others that a team is "#1." Ours, however, is an orange hand giving the middle finger salute. It was never successfully justified, in my opinion, but the argument was that our foam fingers were inappropriate for kids in attendance. These are the same kids who were running around pretending to shoot each other with machine guns and playing video games in which you might be decapitated with your spine ripped out of your body. I don't mind following the convention's rules, but at least be consistent.

Summer of Psychology

I've always heard about the "carrot or the stick" idea when it comes to managing. It's closely related to the phrase, "You attract more bees with honey than with vinegar." I'm not sure who is trying to attract flying insects with detachable spikes filled with apitoxin, but the metaphor seems reasonable. With tour managers, it's usually the stick.

For my Managerial Psychology class, I was fortunate enough to discover Henry Levinson while conducting research for my final team project. Levinson was an Organizational Psychologist who developed "The Great Jackass Fallacy." He argued that there is a prevailing managerial assumption that motivation and manipulation are one and the same. Managers all too often treat their employees like crap but offer them simultaneous monetary bonuses to balance it out. They swing the stick with a carrot attached. No wonder occupational turnover is so high. Managers think of their employees as jackasses. Naturally, I wanted to include all of this in the presentation and persuaded the group to do so. This is how I came to repeatedly say "jackass" in a formal graduate presentation and get praised for my work. It was a great moment for academia.

This was around the time I got to meet Dr. Ray Forbes, Program Chair of the Business Psychology program. I had read a few of his published articles for my classes but wanted to put a face to the name. It can be intimidating to visit a person whose office has so many books. Upon me audibly wondering how many books he had in his personal library, he mentioned that most of them are at home. Additionally, these bookshelves were two layers thick. He didn't have enough space for them all with just a single row on each shelf. I recognized many of the authors I had recently come to admire but others were new to me. I need to read more.

Dr. Forbes has a charming way of communicating. He never assumes you are dumb, so the way he speaks is memorable. I once received an email that began, "Given your busy current and future scheduling, you appear to have become a master at rapid serial task switching." Anyone else would have told me I'm good at multitasking, but he is up on the cognitive research that points out that the idea of multitasking is a myth from a neuroscience perspective. Your conscious attention rapidly flip-flops back and forth; it doesn't process information simultaneously like a multi-core computer processor. Thus, we are task switchers, not multitaskers.

During the visit, we mostly discussed my goals in the program. Every few minutes there was a new concept I wanted to research or a book he recommended I read. I had to start taking notes just to keep up. By the end, I gave him a printed copy of my MEG paper, of which I was particularly proud.

Next up was Behavioral Economics and Neurofinance, which was the course I had been eagerly anticipating for months. I had discovered the work of Dan Ariely a couple of years before, and by the time the class started, I had already read three of his books. He is a researcher at Duke University, and he has not one, but *two* Ph.D.'s to his name. One is in cognitive psychology, and the other in business administration. Does that make him Dr. Dr. Ariely? Naturally, I did my final project for the class on his work and even convinced a few of my classmates to purchase a book or two.

One concept of particular interest to me was explained in Ariely's first book, Predictably Irrational. He explains (much more eloquently than I) that offering two purchasing choices that are relatively different can make it challenging to make a choice. (Let's use the example of a hardcover and a digital version of a book called Dichotomies). However, by adding a third, clearly inferior choice similar to one of the first two choices offers us something to compare. It makes the choice less abstract. It transforms the question from, "Do I want to buy this book?" into "Which version shall I buy?"

If Dichotomies is available on the Psychostick merch store as a deluxe hardcover for $24.99 with a free digital copy, and the hardcover alone is available for the same price, the sole hardcover is clearly inferior. Meanwhile, even if the digital copy is priced much lower at $9.99, it still seems like a bad deal (even if $9.99 is around the market price of a comparable book).

Meanwhile, an inescapable fact of the modern publishing world is that around 40% of all book sales come from Amazon.com (nearly 90% for eBooks). Thus, neglecting to list Dichotomies on Amazon would be a huge mistake on my part. However, since I have less control over pricing on Amazon than I do via Psychostick, it is critical to offer a paperback version as well. A medium-priced paperback may seem like a great deal relative to the more expensive hardcover, even though it is listed around the market price of a similar paperback. What effect do you think the pricing structure had on your decision to purchase Dichotomies? Are you holding a hardcover or paperback in your hands, or did you opt for an eBook?

Presentation by an English Dumpster

I was pretzeled up in the rear bunk of the minibus struggling to participate in a conference call with my final presentation teammates five time zones away. As our very German driver "FREEEEDAAA" meandered down the English countryside, all I needed was a 15-minute window to practice my part. 10 minutes even.

Mercifully, Frieda pulled over for a stop at a petrol station (as they call it in the UK), and I was bequeathed a strong but brief WiFi signal. I quickly jumped in to practice with my team before we had to depart and abandon the scarce but crucial commodity. I had a nagging reservation clawing in my brain. Was I really going to attempt this in front of my professor and classmates tomorrow?

Frieda's minibus parked in a Tesco lot on the first day of the tour.

In the event that I was completely unable to participate, Kooks helped me record my audio for the presentation the week before we left for our second UK tour. I had no intention of letting down my team, but I was also unsure if I could pull this off. We were scheduled to play 17 shows in 19 days all over the island, so there wasn't much room for error.

As luck would have it, the WiFi behind the Live Rooms venue in Chester, England was just fine for my needs. It even felt early after we finished our show[2]. Thankfully, we only had a two-hour drive to Nottingham the following day, so we were parked for the night in the lot behind the club because they were nice enough to provide us with a power cable. The minibus was equipped with shore power, which is how motor vehicles, boats, and even some aircraft plug in to the grid rather than idle their engines all night.

By the time the presentation time arrived at 8:30 Eastern, it was 1:30 in the morning for me. Flanked by empty kegs to my right and a dumpster to my left, I could just make out the

---

[2] British concerts are either strangely early or U.S. concerts are dreadfully late.

banging from the Chester Train Station construction workers across the street through my headphones. My Bose headphones are nice, but they don't block out *everything*. Ironically, the presentation was for Psychology of Marketing, and we had chosen to propose a marketing strategy for an a-la-carte cable Internet service. If only they had more extensive service in England. As I hammered on, so did the rail workers. I did my best to imagine the class listening to my words rather than the clanging going on across the street. This would become my new go-to ridiculous story when someone wants to know how I manage to do schoolwork on tour. Sometimes you just have to hang out by a dumpster.

Creepily giving my PSYC 605 final presentation behind a venue.

One of the most important concepts I learned in my marketing class regarded the consistency of logos. As we observe the Universe for some 16 hours each day (a little less if we're lucky), we view our world through a pinhole. Only the center of our vision is in the sharp clarity we like to think of as eyesight. Everything else that surrounds that point is somewhat blurred.

To compensate, our thoughtful brains use a fancy strategy that makes our eyeballs bounce around from object to object, several times a second. These jitters are known as saccades. "Then why doesn't the world look jerky?" you might ask. Our brains compensate by anticipating each saccadic eye movement and adjusting our perception accordingly to make our vision clear and smooth. This is why clear, distinct logos are so important.

This is one of the reasons you can so easily browse the aisles of a grocery store without purposefully staring at each item individually. You instantly know when you enter the laundry detergent aisle by the distinct green and red Gain jugs and the colorful target Tide packaging. These companies don't have a monopoly on color, but they do understand that consistent logos and color schemes allow you to subconsciously detect their products before you are even aware of it.

Bands use the same strategy. Think about the Nine Inch Nails logo, or Hatebreed, or Slipknot. Each of these groups feature distinctive, consistent branding on their albums and merch. If you are a fan of Meshuggah, you know their bold, all caps logo. It might be interlaced with serpents or sculpted out of stone, but you will never see it in cursive.

In fact, lots of bands do a great job with this. Perusing through my collection I see Alkaline Trio, Chevelle, Darkane, Dillinger Escape Plan, The Faint, Machine Head, Norma Jean, Pig Destroyer, Transplants, and Zebrahead, to name a few standouts. Take a look at your own music collection. Which band logos do you consider to be unmistakable and iconic?

Goldfinger is another great band with one of my favorite logos. The group has used slight variations on the classic version debuted on the self-titled album (1996), then on Hang-Ups (1997), Stomping Ground (2000), and Open Your Eyes (2002). Then they did something weird and put out Disconnection Notice (2005) with the band name in stencils and a GF circle underneath it. It's a good album, but the cover didn't feel like Goldfinger to me. Fortunately, they brought back the classic look for Hello Destiny (2008). Most recently, they returned with my favorite work from them in years on the album The Knife (2017). It features the preeminent Travis Barker on drums, but they used yet another new logo.

Similarly, my own band's logo has evolved over the years as well. What began as a somewhat rounded logo in the early years of the group has developed into a much blockier design in its most recent iteration. However, the design itself has remained fairly consistent overall. Consider the Psychostick discography on the following page:

2006

2007

2009

2011

2014

2018

Did you notice anything strange? Take a look at our 2009 release, Sandwich, a second time. While all the others feature the distinguishable hooks on the "P" and the "K" of the logo, Sandwich did not. I can't help but wonder how much this has hindered our sales of the album over the years. Maybe one day we will re-release it with two more squirts of ketchup to fix the blunder.

The first week of my next course was also the final week of the UK tour. Possibly the wildest show of the tour was in London, at the oddly named Boston Music Room. Just before taking the stage, Matty had us pause and reflect. It was a special moment. The place was packed, and we were headlining in London, England on our second trip to the UK, but this time for three whole weeks. We even added a new country on this trip; we had played Swansea and Cardiff in Wales just a few days earlier.

As great as the trip had been, I was eager to get back to work to finish my degree. The next class was Psychology of Human Resources. This one got me a bit heated. It wasn't the study of motivational factors, workplace stressors, or member retention, it was the final presentation. There was a seeming lack of scientific credibility with the subject, and it was driving me crazy. It had to do with generational differences in the workplace.

Frankly, I can get a bit irritated when I hear that tired, recycled allegation that "millennials are lazy." It's just a stereotype, and it is not based on scientific evidence, as far as I can tell. Why on Earth were we studying this baloney in a Master of Science class? Rather than complain, I decided to go all in. I did my part and found substantial evidence to suggest that the whole concept of generations is inherently flawed.

For instance, generational groups are not even taken from

consistent spans of time. Further, the times may be different depending on whom you ask. What some call "Millennials" might describe people born between 1980-2000 or 1982-2002 or 1980-1999. Even if each group was taken from a consistent 20-year duration of time, there is still a glaring, unsolvable issue. Each group is observed at a different stage of life. The groups are of different ages, grew up in different socioeconomic circumstances, are typically at different points in their careers and family dynamics, and so on. With so many confounding variables, generational studies are correlational at *best*.

In the present day, "Baby Boomers" are said to be goal-oriented, focused, disciplined, and have a strong work ethic. However, we are looking at a group of people from our current, modern perspective. How different might these stereotypes be when viewed from their parents when these Boomers were considered "hippies" in the 1960s? They would probably be called lazy and entitled.

I'm predicting it right now. In a couple of decades, the Millennials will be calling the next group the same thing, and we will have forgotten all about how society is denigrating them in the present day. It's just a cycle of grumpy old people making condescending remarks about young people. Anyone can dig up anecdotal data to support what they want to believe. That's not science or journalism. That's confirmation bias.

After my team presented on the "Generation X" cohort, I called BS. Our professor asked which generation is the most likely to be respectable, trustworthy, and generally a good hire. I jumped right in and verbally lambasted the entire generational pile of garbage. I argued that the concept of generations is just a pretentious way for people to stigmatize others (which is also known as prejudice). It's all nonsense, and I said as much, albeit in a much more professional tone. There was silence for a few moments before he chimed back in. That was exactly what he wanted us to learn all along. I was floored. We had spent weeks compiling flawed information to present, only to learn it was all a long con. Well played, professor.

That was about it for shows in 2016. We had a weeklong run down to Dallas for a festival, but that was pretty much it. I was clear to focus solely on my studies. Finally, the last class for the year was one I had been eagerly anticipating, Psychology of Creativity, Innovation, & Change. It was a fascinating exploration into the numerous facets of creativity in the workplace and entrepreneurship.

I also became the unofficial leader of the class because I'm an active participant in a "creative industry" as a musician. I shared my peculiar perspective about various topics and strived to express the idea that everyone can be creative; it is not a finite resource rationed out to a few lucky members of society. In fact, it's the opposite. We all begin creative as children, but gradually mold ourselves to reflect whatever others expect of us. We only learn that it's "inappropriate" or "incorrect" later in life. Your capacity for creativity is limited solely by you.

CHAPTER 2017

 The comment was reminiscent of my first encounter with Mushroomhead, but this time by a polite Swedish person on tour in the U.S. for the first time. It was Niklas Karvonen from Machinae Supremacy. His band was touring with URIZEN and Danimal Cannon, but we were invited to play two of their shows in Illinois and Indiana. He asked, "What are you working on?"

Niklas was interested in the Psychology of Organizational Coaching[1] paper I was composing because he too was in graduate school. Although his studies were currently on hiatus to tour with his band, he was wrapping up this Ph.D. in Pervasive and Mobile Computing at Luleå University of Technology[2].

This was the first time I had met someone who was juggling

---

[1] My first class as a Psychology professor at Franklin University would be the undergrad version of this class, PSYC 325 - Coaching in Organizations in 2019.

[2] Dr. Niklas Karvonen now researches wearable devices and machine learning.

musical and educational responsibilities. We excitedly shared stories and academic interests, albeit briefly. His band had a half-joking rule of "no dissertation talk on tour," probably to maintain the sanity of the other band members. It can be all-consuming, which probably gets tedious for others if you can't stop bringing up your research.

Setting Goals and Rock 'n Roll

The final class of my master's degree would be Business Psychology Mastery Demonstration in February and March of 2017. Fittingly, we had two shows booked with Ventana the weekend before the class began. It was satisfying to see them again at that point because it felt like a full circle.

The looming thesis paper had been on my mind for months. I wished to pursue a topic that was interesting enough to get me through the entirety of the project. Thus, my peer coach[3] helped me narrow down my thesis topic to the subject of goal setting. I originally wanted to study both goal setting as well as motivation, but quickly realized it would become more of an exhaustive exposition than a compelling thesis. In any case, I had been piling on increasingly outlandish goals for several years now, so why not study it formally?

My thesis idea was that the way goals are framed could impact the success achieved by the goal maker. For instance, a professor's positively framed goal of, "I want to be granted tenure" would be more effective than the negatively framed goal, "I want to avoid being denied tenure." That was the idea, but I needed evidence.

As research takes time to conduct, I decided to collect some preliminary data while still completing the previous class. To

---

[3] A big part of Psychology of Organizational Coaching was conducting actual coaching sessions with a student peer.

do this, I conducted a pair of surveys concerning New Year's resolutions using the online tool, Survey Monkey. I asked my participants, "Do you or did you have a New Year's resolution for 2017?" About a third of my nearly 800 participants responded that yes, they had made a resolution this year. That was interesting, but not my primary objective. I wanted to know how these people framed goals in their own words, and how that compared to their self-reported goal attainment so far. To get that information without giving away the whole concept (and skew the data), I mixed in a few demographic questions. However, the most important question inquired about the participants' goals in their own words. Then the attainment was rated on a scale between 0-100, asking "Provided you made a resolution, how successful have you been with your objective?" It wasn't a perfect study, not by a long shot. But it was the best I knew how to do at the time. You have to start somewhere.

As I combed through the responses, I found several interesting themes. First, there was no significant difference in reported goal attainment between gender, age, education, number of languages spoken, or even how many musical instruments the person plays on a regular basis. Next, I coded the goals and how they were framed by looking at the verbs they chose to use. If the words used were constructive or productive verbs such as *accomplish, get, obtain, achieve, better, improve,* and *start,* they were determined to be framed positively. On the other hand, goals describing inhibition or obstruction such as *lose, less, stop, never,* and *quit* were considered to be framed negatively. Finally, any goals with multiple objectives and conflicting frames were classified as neutral.

To be clear, this is not a peer-reviewed academic study that I am describing. It was merely a semi-formal correlational survey I conducted to obtain evidence for my central hypothesis. However, I did find some corroborating evidence in a study published by Drs. Chris Roney and Darrin Lehman, which I incorporated into my thesis to strengthen the argument. Additionally, I discovered the seminal goal setting work by Drs. Edwin Locke and Gary Latham with the advice of my professor, Dr. Kristan Jones. Their central premise is that effective goals should be specific, measurable, and moderately challenging. Of course, that smashes four decades of research into a single sentence, so it's preferable to read the source material.

Composing one's thesis in a room with a crazed man wielding a hammer is not conducive to productivity. Actually, the crazed man was just outside, smashing the window to climb inside. I was visiting Kooks and his admirably tolerant wife, Jen, while putting the final touches on my paper. Meanwhile, Dave Solar, the singer of the band Ideamen, was committing the act of home invasion. It was actually for a music video for the song Deck of Cards, which was being filmed that day by Murph and Kooks as I tried to stay out of the way. (It was also a rubber hammer and a fake window). You can witness the scene in question about a minute into the video. Dave climbs through the window and walks by the dining table I had occupied just minutes before.

Despite the ongoing theme of hammers, I did, in fact, complete the thesis. In fact, while researching the many facets of goal setting, I came across several concepts that can apply directly to musicians and other artists. I decided to blend my goal-related ideas with the music world to offer a compelling, real-world application of the various concepts.

One concept relates to primary and sub-goals. Primary goals represent the true objective of the goal setter and are ends in themselves. To accomplish a given primary goal, a person must typically achieve several sub-goals that add up to the ultimate primary goal. In my case, I had to complete a number of papers to successfully complete my classes, and finish classes to earn my degrees. While a single paper may be interesting to compose, it doesn't often have a ton of value in isolation. However, focusing on sub-goals has been shown to be more motivating because minor setbacks may be attributed to individual sub-goals rather than the larger scope primary goal. Getting a crappy grade on a single assignment does not doom the entire endeavor.

I applied the concept of sub-goals directly to the music recording process. Focusing solely on the end product (a complete album) can be daunting, to put it mildly. Songs must be conceptualized, demoed, tweaked, rehearsed, tracked, mixed, mastered, and then packaged with appropriate artwork and liner notes to be released as an album. It can take months if a band is lightning fast, or in the case of the band Tool, over a decade to release a record.

A practical application here is to create a physical grid on paperboard with song titles on one axis and tasks to complete on another. Drawings or stickers may be added to each cell as the tasks are gradually completed. It can be quite exciting to visually observe the progress of the album over the days, weeks, and months as it nears completion.

There is another fascinating concept that I came across in one of Dan Ariely's books known as hedonic adaptation. Simply put, we become used to things over time. One study discovered that there is essentially a base level of happiness in people that remains fairly consistent over time for individuals. After a few months, lottery winners come down from the initial high of hitting it big and return to their personal average happiness level. Similarly, paralyzed accident victims tend to climb up out of their initial depression from the massive setback. People tend to become accustomed to their circumstances.

Superficially, you could use this concept to help promote small happiness boosts. If house renovating is your thing, don't fix everything at once. Replace the blinds, then buy the couch set a few months later, then get the new carpet, and so on. Buying a Ferrari will only make you happy for a little while until you get used to it. You'd probably be just as happy with a reliable Honda in the long run.

I used the idea of hedonic adaptation to present an innovative way for bands to release music. First, I explained the album cycle that most bands go through every few years. To oversimplify it, bands typically write songs, record songs, press albums, release albums, tour extensively to support the album, and repeat it all a few years later. Rather than release all that music at once, wouldn't it make more sense for the consumers (fans) if artists released music just a little at a time? Although I prefer the CD album format (and the cool artwork and packaging that comes along with it), many people do not. That said, my personal preference for music consumption is irrelevant in this case.

Imagine an innovative group that releases one song paired with a music video each month, *forever* (or at least as long as the group remains together). The band would need to be prolific and write new material regularly, but it is certainly viable. Consider the possibilities. The industry currently operates using the 1:1 transaction model, as I call it, in which an album is released and there is a binary outcome. Either fans purchase that album, or they do not. Even if they do purchase the current release, it may be challenging to keep the attention of your fanbase with new material coming only every few years. Alternatively, offering music on a subscription basis could entice fans to commit to paying, let's say, $1 each month, so $12/year. I spend more than that on things I hate, like toll roads. Why wouldn't I spend that tiny amount on an artist I admire? What if a band has 1,000 fans willing to participate? What about 10,000?

I had an audience of one for this project: Dr. Jones. As far as I know, she does not have a background in the music business. Regardless, it was a compelling thought exercise. Months of work had culminated in my master's thesis, which I opted to name Setting Goals and Rock 'n Roll. On the big day that I was to present my work to the class, I received an email from the university's Provost, Dr. Christopher Washington. It was a cordial invitation to represent Franklin University as the graduate speaker at the commencement ceremony in May. He just happened to send his invitation the same day I was supposed to present my findings from months of work on my paper in the graduate program. Dr. Forbes must be the culprit who set this in motion.

I would be lying if I said I wasn't flustered. I opted to confirm that yes, I would be honored to speak. That allowed me to corral my thoughts somewhat. At least I didn't have to consider which decision to make any longer. It was already made. It was an exciting prospect, however, so I privately shared the news with Dr. Jones. She replied, "Now I am really expecting big things." No pressure.

It's funny the things we remember and the things we forget. You would think I'd remember giving my presentation to the class, which represented 14 months of graduate work. I don't. What I do remember is what happened after all the students were finished. Dr. Jones declared, "One of your peers has a big announcement to make, but I didn't ask permission to tell you about it. Let's see if we can get a confession." I sheepishly chimed in and paraphrased the request from Dr. Washington. The word was out, and I couldn't help but shake my head at the absurdity of it all.

The final show of my graduate career took place at Grizzly Hall in Austin, Texas. It was April, still a month before my graduation, but all my coursework was complete. All I had to do now was compose a speech. But first, we had a show to perform. The band Anthrax was headlining, one of the "big four" thrash groups. We were in good company. What a fine way to mark another milestone.

Commencement Speech

Zeno's arrow never hits the mark… The lyrics ring in my head like an earworm. No, not an earworm; that's a pejorative. It's a song I love. It moves me. It inspires me to push through and achieve my objective. My hands are trembling, just like the first speech I gave for my friends on tour. I'm about to represent my entire university as the first ever Business Psychology graduate commencement speaker, but my thoughts race back to that book I read by Amy Cuddy. What was the term? Imposter syndrome? That is how I feel to some extent. Am I worthy of such an honor?

I know the objective facts. I have completed 51 courses over the past six years to be sitting here now. I'm a few rows from the front of my graduating class because my last name starts with "D." That means I'll need to awkwardly stumble across the row to get to the side of the stage in a moment. I ball my hands into fists and squeeze as hard as I can for a few moments. It was a trick I had learned in my speech class.

Something to do with nervousness. "And our graduate student commencement speaker's name is…"

I start thinking about the 505 concerts my band had performed since I enrolled in college that very first semester. Personal Finance and Pre-Algebra. 505 concerts in five countries. The other week I had calculated that I performed just over 24% of all the days that have elapsed since my enrollment in 2011. "Alexander is not only a student at Franklin, he is also a musician…" *Zeno's arrow…*

The song chimes on in my head. I'm now at the side of the stage preparing to climb the stairs and approach the lectern. I strive to focus on being calm, but my mind keeps harping on about everything that has happened. 246 shows while I pursued my associate's. 216 during my bachelor's. A mere 43 in the past 14 months during my enrollment in the master's program. None of these people would ever know these numbers.

People are clapping. Move. I'm suddenly on stage, but I don't remember walking over. I vaguely recall shaking someone's hand, but once again I have no idea what that person said to me. I look down at my script as I prepare to speak and try to steady myself. I recognize the words in the top right corner of the page. *Right. That's why I have that song in my head.* The words are lyrics from a song by Dessa. I had scribbled a line from "Fighting Fish" in the top right corner.

None of the things going through my head are in the actual speech I'm about to deliver. It's about overcoming obstacles, not showing off what I had done. Franklin students are primarily working adults, like me, and I wanted to do our collective efforts justice. My hands are on the top edges of the lectern now, half to steady myself and half to prevent me from waving my arms around nervously. I glance down to my script and read Dessa's words.

"I make my own luck now."

Speeches are all about cadence and timing. It's not unlike drumming. I have more than enough experience to pull this off if I think about it that way. I begin with an idiom to introduce the idea that we're all busy people. There is always something more to do, to pursue, to accomplish. Sometimes life gets in the way of our goals. But if you don't start on them now, when will you? I wasn't ready to give up touring when I decided to pursue this goal, so I didn't.

Wrapping up a speech with, "Congratulations, graduates!" is always a surefire way to score some applause. However, this is no time to stall. It's time to load off stage so the next artist, or in this case, speaker, can shine. Although I feel fairly certain Dr. Washington will be shaking his head at my weird performance, we suddenly make eye contact for a brief moment. He is giving me a thumbs up! I hadn't disappointed Franklin University after all.

Making Franklin University proud.
From left to right: Josh, me, Rob, & Matty.

TO BE CONTINUED

There is nothing quite like a prop that reads, "Album Release Button" to make people lose their minds and want to smash it. It has been a year since I graduated with my master's degree, and I have spent the time gradually introducing new psychological concepts into the inner business practices of my band. Well, in this case the large red and gray button is anything but subtle. It is now the 24th of July on a Tuesday evening in 2018. No one had a clue until a few moments before, but we are about to unleash our new album "DO" to the world live on a webcast.

In case you have no idea how the music industry operates, this strategy is the exact opposite of conventional thinking. First, it was a Tuesday. Although albums used to be released on Tuesdays in the U.S., Canada and the UK put out albums on Mondays, while Australia and Germany released them on Fridays. Then in 2015, the music industry adopted a global standard—everything is released on Fridays from now on. In my completely biased opinion based solely on sentimental attachment, I think the change sucks. I have numerous fond memories of franticly anticipating new releases at Zia Records[1] on Tuesdays growing up. Plus, DO has a song about how awesome Tuesdays are. Although the line didn't make the final cut, we originally intended to point out that I, your author, was born on a Tuesday.

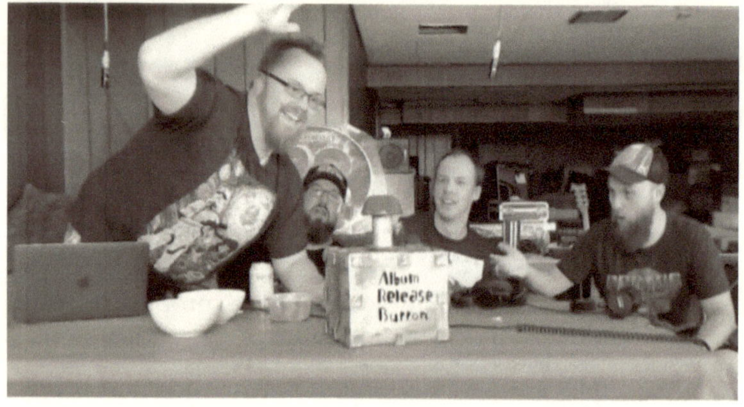

Rob about to release "DO" to the world.

The other bizarre strategy we decided to experiment with was a complete disregard of the idea of an album pre-order. You simply cannot get away with this unless your group is a) massive enough to control your own career despite your record label warning you against it, or b) you have independent control, meaning you don't have a label dictating your career at all.

While Psychostick was signed to Rock Ridge Music (RRM) from 2006-2017, we had grown in different directions. I will be forever grateful for the professionalism and honesty of the people at RRM. It's a wonderful company and I wish them the

____

[1] Zia Records warrants a trip to Arizona or Nevada.

very best. However, we wanted to tinker with the conventional marketing strategies. Labels are generally not known for their adaptability in that regard.

We had decided to release DO abruptly on a webcast for several reasons. First, it gave us the element of surprise. We had been around for 18 years at that point, and our fans have been through the album announcement/pre-order/release process over and over. It's not a bad model, but it isn't particularly interesting either.

There is a concept known as a hot-cold empathy gap that describes how people act when their emotions are elevated. It relates to all kinds of things, from sexual desire to purchasing decisions. It's the reason why couples accidentally get pregnant, and why you might pay $14 for a hot fudge sundae on a date but would refuse to spend more than $4 on a whole carton of ice cream at a grocery store. In a hot state, people are simply more interested in immediate gratification.

It also relates to preferences. Sudden tour announcements are exciting, especially with alluring tour artwork. When I discover new tour dates for a band I like, I often become very excited and purchase tickets for the show right away. However, my preference for the same exact tour is diminished if I hear about a tour but don't buy tickets immediately. It's the same band; it's the same tour; the difference is the hot-cold empathy gap. This is the reason why it is vital for bands to provide ticket links for concerts at the same time the tour is announced. The same goes for albums.

Releasing a pre-order for an album doesn't make any sense to me if the purchaser doesn't get any immediate gratification. Why would I pre-order a CD when I won't get to hear it for two more months? I could just wait…and in waiting my interest quickly declines. It's not that people are uncaring.

Music lovers, by and large, want to support artists. People greatly enjoy the gratification of knowing they are directly funding something important and inspiring to them. There is just so much media grasping for attention these days. A pre-order may simply get lost in the noise.

Thus, we promised immediate gratification with our album, DO. In a way, I envy the people who love Psychostick and got to experience the rush of a brand-new album suddenly becoming available in that very moment. The huge red and gray "Album Release Button" promised much more than a pre-order. It offered the immediate chance to purchase and download the entire album, right then and there. Every CD came with a digital copy. Many of the people even opted to log out of the webcast to listen to the new album instead. "Should we press it?" The comments began flooding in like a raging river.

"I don't know. Maybe they don't want a new album." *PRESS THE BUTTON! We can't wait any longer! I'm dying! For the love of god, press the button!* Now *that* is a hot state.

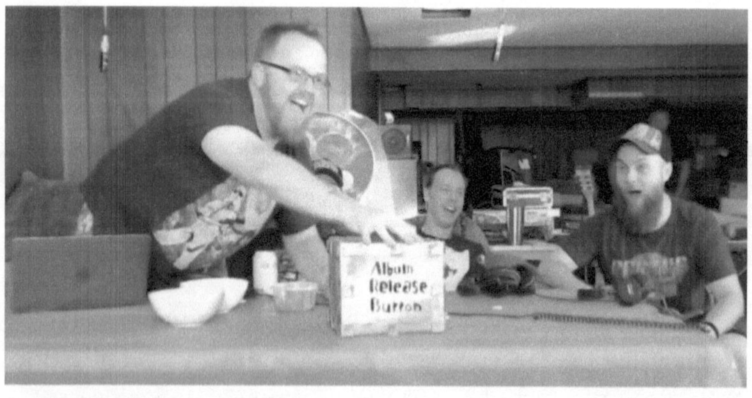

Dichotomies

Dichotomies are a big part of my bizarre life. For instance, my band plays *comedy* metal. I earned my degrees on *tour* while I studied. My Master's is in Business *Psychology*. Even my musical preferences are a bit odd. Some of my favorite groups beautifully sing intricate harmonies, such as Dessa and Punch Brothers. Some other favorites of mine offer a sonic assault on the senses such as the Dillinger Escape Plan. In 2017, my band played Dragon Con in Atlanta and gave a shout-out to the furries in the audience. A few months later, we performed on the 70,000 Tons of Metal cruise with the likes of Cannibal Corpse and Meshuggah.

I suppose this is why I choose to live such a strange, mismatched life. It makes things seem more interesting to me when other people are confused. If I meet someone new who asks me what I do for a living or what I am researching, I don't want them to immediately understand. It's just more fun to be the oddball.

As I complete this project in October of 2019, I have something to confess to you, my dear reader. I have been accepted into a doctoral program. I intend to keep up my unusual habit of juggling multiple projects at once. Music, education, research. I enjoy them all, so I plan to continue with each. I might study the psychology of decision making. Perhaps habit formation and cessation. Maybe even neuroeconomics. Regardless, I'm sure I will approach it from a strange vantage point. I also know I am being a little vague, but I have to save *something* for the sequel. Maybe I'll call it *Dichotomies II: The Curse of the Doctoral Thesis.*

APPENDIX A:
SPEECH TRANSCRIPTION

*Given at the Franklin University Graduation Ceremony
on the 19th of May 2017*

Greetings, graduates, faculty, friends, and family! Thank you for the introduction.

I imagine most of the people in this room have heard the idiom, "when it rains, it pours." Personally, I detect a mild hint of negativity in the phrase, so I prefer something my friend Paul once told me. "You don't have to shovel rain." In any case, when it rains, it does often seem to pour, as good things seem to occur in groups. For instance, when our distinguished Provost, Dr. Washington, offered me the honor to speak at this very ceremony, he sent the invitation on the same day as my final presentation for the Business Psychology capstone! Naturally, I was quite astounded and shared the wonderful news with my instructor, Dr. Jones. Of course, she congratulated me and mentioned that she looked forward to my presentation that evening, then casually slipped in, "now I am really expecting big things." When it rains, it pours.

However, why is it that we tend to notice things in clumps, whether good or bad? I recently did some research about that in the realm of behavioral economics. Now, it's really not as dreadful as it sounds. It's really quite interesting. For instance, we have the availability heuristic. It has a fancy sounding name, but the idea is actually pretty simple. It describes how people tend to make judgments about the likelihood of an event or occurrence based on how easily an example comes to mind. Recent car buyers suddenly start noticing their model all over the roads. We see what we expect to see, and often overlook what we do not expect.

So, what do you expect from a well-dressed graduate speaker going on about behavioral biases? A year ago, I earned a degree in finance, so I'm not a betting man. But if I were, I would wager that most of you might consider me an upstanding citizen—one you might invite to a prestigious social gathering. What you probably wouldn't guess is that I am also a drummer in a metal band called Psychostick. That's right—they didn't get the memo that you're not supposed to let the drummer in front of a microphone to speak! Nevertheless, here I am, and I have a rather bizarre story to share.

Last September I was enrolled in the Psychology of Marketing course while simultaneously touring in the UK. Indeed, during the final two weeks of the class, I was gallivanting around the island to play 17 shows in 19 days. Fortunately, there is a 5-hour time difference between Eastern and British Standard Time. On the infamous night of September 15, 2016, we had an early performance and wrapped things up by around 10 p.m. local time. Fortunately, the venue provided our minibus with a power cord that evening, so we were able to sleep behind the club—luxurious, I know. Soon, it was 2 am British Time (which made it 9 pm Eastern the night before), and the moment had arrived. I was able to set up by a dumpster in an English alley behind a bar to present with my remarkably patient peers, Danae and Scott. When it rains, it pours!

If I had to offer one small piece of advice, it would be this: embrace the uncertainty that comes with a challenging scenario. You might surprise some people with what you are able to accomplish. Better yet, you just might surprise yourself. Thank you so much for the opportunity to speak this evening.

It has been quite an honor to be a student of Franklin University for the past few years. I especially wish to thank the incredible faculty, staff, instructors, and all of my supportive friends who helped me retain my sanity, if not a semblance of normalcy. I wish all of you the best.

Congratulations, graduates!

APPENDIX B: MASTER'S THESIS

Setting Goals and Rock 'n Roll
Submitted to Dr. Kristan Jones on the 28th of March 2017

Executive Summary

What is a goal, and how can one improve his or her goal setting proficiency? The current project begins with a discussion about the importance of setting goals and then examines Locke and Latham's prominent theory. Goal setting theory makes several key observations and recommendations, such as to set moderately challenging, specific goals. The high-performance cycle, a subset of the theory, is then considered. There is also a distinction made between performance goals (attainment) and mastery goals (learning). Once the appropriate type of goal is selected, it can be beneficial to emphasize sub-goals rather than strictly focus on overarching primary goals. The implications of organizational goal setting are also explored.

The next section builds on goal setting with an analysis of several key behavioral economics principles. It begins with the seminal concept of prospect theory developed by Kahneman and Tversky. The inherent sensitivity to losses offers significant implications for effective goal setting. It also explores the effects of hedonic adaptation and how people adapt to novel stimuli over time. Goal setters with knowledge of this behavioral quirk have a distinct advantage that encourages improved goal setting and behavior. Finally, the concept of goal framing is examined and tested using two surveys conducted in early 2017. The results confirm the general hypothesis; goals with positive framing result in higher self-reported success rates than do goals with negative framing.

Many of the investigated concepts are then applied to the author's organization in the form of a thought experiment. There are numerous ways in which to apply the recommendations, but there are unique strengths for when to apply each strategy. Accordingly, different operational modes of the organization offer varied opportunities to apply the goal setting principles.

Introduction

An ambitious physicist might impose a personal goal to determine the veracity of the big-bang model by detecting elusive gravitational waves emitted from the purported inflationary period some 13.8 billion years ago (Paulson, Albert, Holt, & Turok, 2015). Simultaneously, that same person might perennially chase simpler goals, such as arriving to work on time. With such a wide variety in the scope, difficulty, and even the need for conscious deliberation, how might one define a goal? Goal setting theorists, Locke and Latham (2002), suggest, "A goal is the object or aim of an action, for example, to attain a specific standard of proficiency, usually within a specified time limit" (p. 705). Alternatively, Elliot and Fryer (2008) propose, "A goal is a cognitive representation of a future object that the organism is committed to approach or avoid" (p. 245).

The goal of the author is to compose a compelling, informative paper that does not result in inopportune fatigue or irritability of the reader. To focus the inherently expansive topic to something manageable, it will target personal and organizational goals that exist in the realm of business psychology. The aim is to explore current theories about goals and to provide recommendations with useful ways in which to improve goal performance. Goal setting theory advocated by Locke and Latham will be considered to accomplish these tasks. Next, various behavioral economics concepts will be introduced that might assist or discourage successful goal setting. One of the behavioral concepts will then be examined further with two surveys conducted in early 2017. The various concepts will be synthesized and applied to the author's organization, including recommendations based on the insights developed throughout the project. Finally, there will be a brief summary of the author's personal takeaways that relate to improved goal setting and a general conclusion about the overall project.

Goal Setting Theory

Since it was developed nearly half a century ago, goal setting theory has blossomed into one of the most influential and useful models in the history of behavioral science (Locke & Latham, 2002). It is also one of the most thoroughly tested in an empirical sense, with over 1,000 studies conducted with 40,000+ participants across the globe (Latham & Locke, 2007; Locke & Latham, 2006). The theory may be summarized as predicting that an individual will be more productive by setting a specific, moderately challenging goal, rather than a vague goal or none at all (Locke, Shaw, Saari, & Latham, 1981).

While a recommendation to set a "challenging" goal might seem subjective to the individual, the evidence gathered to test the theory shows that performance improves with increasing difficulty, up to a point (Locke & Latham, 2002). One might graph the task performance rate with an upside-down letter "U," with effortless goals and acutely arduous goals resulting in poorer performance; moderate goal difficulty thus results in peak performance. To explain the variation in perceived difficulty, researchers apply the concept of self-efficacy which describes self-confidence about the task at hand (Latham & Locke, 2007). Congruent with goal setting theory, increased self-efficacy is positively related to motivation, and thus, goal attainment (Bandura & Locke, 2003).

Motivation is closely related to goal attainment. Thus, it is important to consider the disparity between low-level drives (concerned with basic physiological needs), and higher-level drives that contribute to explicit goals (Sun, 2009). However, high and low-level drives often conflict, such as a dieter tempted by a delectable slice of The Cheesecake Factory® Chocolate Tower Truffle Cake[1] (Nutrition Facts, 2009). Instead of treating our future selves with the same consideration as our current selves, we often discount our long-term goals for short-term pleasure, known as hyperbolic time discounting (Berns, Laibson, & Loewenstein, 2007).

Researchers have shown that subconscious drivers can be helpful with conscious goals as well. For instance, when primed with motivational pictures in the workplace, employees have been shown to increase performance, giving conscious and subconscious goals a cumulative effect provided the goals are compatible (Latham, Stajkovic, & Locke, 2010). Related studies offered similar results, but noted that the goals must be context-specific, meaning related to the task at hand (Latham & Piccolo, 2012).

Another subset of goal setting theory is known as the high-performance cycle (HPC) and relates to the productivity of employees in an organizational setting. HPC describes the progression of how moderately high goals lead to improved

---

[1] One serving of this cake delivers an impressive 1,680 calories.

organizational performance, which then contributes to employee rewards and increased self-efficacy (Locke & Latham, 2002). Perhaps counterintuitively, job satisfaction does not directly link to high performance. Instead, employee satisfaction results in greater commitment to the organization, which increases the likelihood of the employee to set high goals (Latham & Locke, 2007). Once high goals are established, there is a virtuous cycle of high performance, increased rewards, enhanced satisfaction, and greater engagement of future challenges.

Performance Goals

There are two basic varieties of achievement goals, defined by Rawsthorne and Elliot (1999) as "the purpose of or reason for competence-relevant activity" (p. 326). The first form is known as a performance goal and is related to an intrinsic target or the extrinsic expectations of others (Elliot & Church, 1997). By measuring goal attainment against a certain standard, a given level of competence is assumed. However, there are sub-classifications of performance goals as well. Performance-approach goals may be described as goals set with the intention of attaining "favorable judgments of competence" from others (Elliot & Church, 1997, p. 218). Alternatively, performance-avoidance describes the evasion of unfavorable judgments. While each form has its advantages, there is evidence that performance-avoidance goals can diminish intrinsic motivation if the goal is simply to avoid failure (Elliot & Harackiewicz, 1996). Accordingly, performance goals are typically more effective when the individual has at least a base level of knowledge and confidence, and therefore adequate self-efficacy about the task (Seijts & Latham, 2005).

Mastery Goals

If the individual has not yet had a chance to develop the skills necessary for effective performance goal setting, mastery goals will likely be more practical. Mastery goals (sometimes called learning goals), focus on the development of competency rather than fixate on task performance (Elliot & Church, 1997). These goals assist in developing self-efficacy, which in turn leads to higher motivation and persistence by helping newcomers to focus their attention. In turn, this helps increase knowledge and efficiency because the individual is not blindly striving to outperform with limited understanding of how to accomplish a task (Seijts & Latham, 2005).

Primary and Sub Goals

Once the appropriate form for the goal is selected, a goal setter has several other opportunities that may help to increase the likelihood of success. For instance, there is evidence of a relationship between motivation and a person's focus on either primary or sub-goals (sometimes called distal or proximal goals, respectively). Primary goals represent the true objective of the goal setter and are ends in themselves (Houser-Marko & Sheldon, 2008). To accomplish a given primary goal, a person typically must achieve a number of sub-goals that add up to the ultimate primary goal. These sub-goals exist for the purpose of accomplishing a larger objective but often have little value in isolation. However, focusing on sub-goals has been shown to be more motivating because minor setbacks may be attributed to individual sub-goals rather than the larger scope primary goal (Houser-Marko & Sheldon, 2008). While potentially motivating, there is evidence that goal setters immersed in a sub-goal may prefer finishing the minor task when nearing completion, even if it threatens the attainment of the primary goal (Ji Hoon & Lynch, 2014). Accordingly, it is important to be cognizant of potential achievement perils, even if they originate from pure intentions.

Organizational Goals

Goal setting in an organization also has several relevant variables. For instance, goals are often assigned by managers rather than independently by subordinates. Goal setting theory predicts that allowing employees to set their own targets would help with motivation because there is a sense of ownership of the objective in mind (Locke & Latham, 2002). However, there is also evidence that assigning goals may be just as effective, provided the managers do not simply instruct employees to engage in an undertaking with no explanation of why it should be pursued (Locke & Latham, 2002).

Once the goal has been established, feedback is an important component to moderation and tracking progress throughout a project (Locke & Latham, 2006). Notwithstanding, it is critical for managers to take care when offering feedback, especially when it may be perceived as negative criticism. Negative feedback given to an employee with high self-efficacy may result in higher subsequent goals, but an employee with lower self-efficacy may be discouraged by the feedback and reduce future effort (Locke & Latham, 2002). Additionally, there is evidence to suggest that progress certainty is related to performance. When the distance to completion of a task is uncertain, discrete progress markers (DPM) can help to reduce the uncertainty, thus improving motivation and performance; when certainty is high, DPM can be detrimental to performance by generating complacency (Amir & Ariely, 2008).

Many goals in the workplace are not set by individuals or managers, but rather by groups of employees. Predictably, when individual goals are aligned with those of the group, the overall group performance is enhanced; when individual and group goals are not aligned, it can be detrimental to group performance (Locke & Latham, 2002). With goals aligned, workers can boost collective performance by working together. However, developing goals as a group, known as participative decision making (PDM), was not found to be a direct cause of improved performance; instead, PDM was shown to increase self-efficacy and task competence which in turn helped to improve performance (Latham & Pinder, 2005). The boost in self-efficacy and competence increased organizational commitment, which is a key element to the HPC theory described above.

Finally, there is a link between motivational factors and self-construal, "typically defined as how individuals see the self in relation to others" (Cross, Hardin, & Gercek-Swing, 2011, p. 143). People with an independent self-construal (IndSC) perspective value autonomy and individual advancement, while a more interdependent self-construal (InterSC) perspective emphasizes socially-oriented accomplishments (Cross, Hardin, & Gercek-Swing, 2011). Employees with an IndSC perspective will likely be more motivated by attainment goals, meaning objectives that help advance the individual in some way; those with an InterSC perspective are usually more motivated by maintenance goals, which maintain a desired state or status level (Yang, Stamatogiannakis, & Chattopadhyay, 2015).

Behavioral Economics

Once a person sets a goal, the traditional economics perspective claims that he or she will behave rationally and make optimal choices to achieve the objective (Thaler, 2016). In contrast, behavioral economists have developed a series of models describing these idealistic agents as Econs—inspired by the economics professors who allegedly believe they exist in society—and everyone else as Humans (Thaler & Sunstein, 2008). Econs make unbiased choices with infinite willpower that increase their personal utility. Humans, on the other hand, are susceptible to a vast array of subtle, perhaps even humorous quirks. Three behavioral economics concepts related to goal setting include prospect theory, hedonic adaptation, and framing.

Prospect Theory

One of the first significant examples of Humans making consistently irrational choices is detailed by Kahneman and Tversky (1979) and is known as prospect theory. The researchers revealed how "losses loom larger than gains" when it comes to decision making, making them risk-averse when it comes to gains but risk-seeking when it comes to potential losses (p. 279).

The perception of goal achievement can also be relative using the prospect theory value function, which is the plotted depiction of loss-aversion. Specifically, the thrill of achieving an objective (and the unpleasantness of failing) is relative to the selected reference point, the goal (Heath, Larrick, & Wu, 1999). An outcome could be perceived as a failure if it does not live up to the reference point, but the same outcome could be a huge success with a lower initial goal.

The value function also predicts a sense of diminishing sensitivity to the reference point. If a goal setter is nowhere near achieving a goal, it is typically much less painful than barely missing the mark. Accordingly, it is much more motivating for a goal setter to push through to achieve a goal when it is just within reach (Heath, Larrick, & Wu, 1999). On the other hand, massively outperforming in relation to the reference point can also reduce motivation to continue, making reasonably high goals an important factor for high performance. Finally, from the prospect theory perspective, goal specificity (as detailed in goal setting theory) could arguably be analogous to goal difficulty, although Locke and Latham would likely disagree with this assertion (Heath, Larrick, & Wu, 1999). From this perspective, a specified goal is presumably more challenging than an ambiguous "do your best" goal, so increasing certainty is simply another way to increase the level of difficulty. It does not conflict with the goal setting theory predictions but instead perceives the traditionally separate variables as one in the same.

Hedonic Adaptation

As mentioned above, hyperbolic time discounting describes the perceived importance of a short-term versus a long-term goal. Similarly, hedonic adaptation describes the modification of perceived pain or pleasure derived from a given stimulus (Frederick & Loewenstein, 1999). It can be used to detail the adaptation to a foul odor over time, the intensity of a painful procedure, and even personal well-being following a personal tragedy or some marvelous event. It relates directly to goal setting because motivational factors can be extremely influential when it comes to persisting with a challenging objective. Independent studies have shown that after just a few months following an event, human beings can adapt to virtually anything. Lottery winners return to the average level of self-reported well-being, just as recently disabled accident victims return to the base level from the opposite direction (Brickman, Coates, & Janoff-Bulman, 1978).

If people are so remarkably adaptive to stimuli, there could be drastic implications to goal setting and motivation. For instance, small, frequent pleasures tend to improve well-being more than large, periodic thrills (Mochon, Norton, & Ariely, 2008). If a person fixates on momentous achievements that may only be realized occasionally, it follows that the triumphs would have only a short-lived effect on overall happiness and well-being due to hedonic adaptation. Instead, focusing on frequent, but minor achievements can improve overall happiness and well-being more effectively if they occur on a regular basis. Accordingly, it aligns with the theory that focusing on sub-goals is typically more motivating than fixating on primary goals.

Finally, experiences seem to be evaluated temporally as "not all information that is unveiled over the course of the experience is weighted equally" (Zauberman, Diehl, & Ariely, 2006, p. 191). The beginning and ending of experiences are typically more indelible than events toward the middle. In fact, researchers have shown that participants often prefer to endure more overall pain as long as the intensity gradually subsides throughout the experience, making it less painful toward the end of the procedure (Ariely, 1998). Similarly, ramping down the intensity of a workout session and finishing with a relatively enjoyable exercise can help to form a more positive memory of the overall experience (Zauberman, Diehl,

& Ariely, 2006). If a goal is to exercise consistently to improve one's health, hedonic adaptation could help increase motivation and persistence, especially regarding future workout sessions. The implications to other seemingly undesirable (but necessary) experiences are extensive, as the method could be used to persevere through numerous challenging goals.

Goal Framing

Predicted by prospect theory, the way in which a doctor frames a diagnosis will likely influence the subsequent decision made by the patient (Kahneman & Tversky, 1984). Offering a 90 percent chance to live versus a 10 percent chance of death will likely result in two different choices. Framing can also influence choices made regarding conflicting short and long-term goals (Berns, Laibson, & Loewenstein, 2007). A marketer might utilize scarcity by highlighting "While supplies last!" to compel an aspiring saver to make an impulsive purchase.

Goals can be framed positively, such as emphasizing greater achievement, or negatively, such as the avoidance of failure. Consequently, the way in which achievement goals are framed could have an effect on personal performance. Several studies tested this idea and concluded that negative framing generally has a detrimental effect on achievement outcomes (Roney & Lehman, 2008). The phenomenon also persisted when researchers offered negatively-framed feedback between a series of exams (Roney & Lehman, 2008). Alternatively, positive feedback framing seems to increase perceived self-efficacy, raise self-set goals, and increase group productivity (Bandura & Locke, 2003). Consequently, goal and feedback framing can have significant effects on both personal and organizational performance.

Researchers have also examined the framing effects on the stress of struggling to achieve a goal. Positively framed, complex performance goals resulted in higher achievement than negatively framed goals that emphasized problematic elements and how the participants could learn to improve over time (Latham & Locke, 2007). Rather than allow goals to be perceived as a threat (if you fail to achieve a particular benchmark, something negative will happen), positive framing adopts a challenge response (Drach-Zahavya & Erez, 2002). The stress of goal setting is thus transformed into an opportunity for self-growth and spurs participants to develop sufficient coping strategies. Applying a challenge response to goals is especially important in organizational settings. Overarching organizational goals influence groups of sub-goals and positive framing seems to be conducive to higher employee motivation, and therefore, value creation (Foss & Lindenberg, 2013).

Framing in Action: Two Surveys

The prevalence of obesity in the U.S. has increased dramatically in the past few decades, from 23 percent in the 1960s to over 36 percent by the early 2010s (Christakis & Fowler, 2007; Ogden, Carroll, Fryar, & Flegal, 2015). It is, therefore, reasonable to conclude that weight reduction is likely a common goal among U.S. adults in modern times. However, recent studies have suggested that the conventional restrictive dieting strategy is ineffective because it frequently leads to intense cravings and overeating (Polivy, Coleman, & Herman, 2005).

Instead, researchers have proposed that switching the focus

from restrictive dieting (negative framing) to overall improved health (positive framing) is more conducive to shedding pounds (Provencher et al., 2009). Additionally, this strategy is also associated with other psychological benefits such as an improved quality of life, increased satisfaction with one's body, and a reduction in binge eating (Gagnon-Girouard et al., 2010). The striking difference in results related to goal framing is the premise of the following two surveys. As expected, roughly 40 percent of the goals related to physical well-being, such as weight management or health.

Survey One

The first online survey was conducted in January of 2017 to provide archival data to study the theory of goal framing. The first selected hypothesis (H1) claimed that the way in which a goal is framed (positively or negatively) would be positively correlated with the self-reported success rates. For instance, a positively framed goal (such as, "I want to improve my health") would result in a higher success rate than a negatively framed goal (such as, "I want to lose 10 pounds"). The survey also coincided with the ritual of declaring a New Year's resolution, which likely enlarged the pool of potential goal-setters.

Of the 769 total participants, 265 provided goals in their own words, with many related to improving habits and achieving specific objectives. The goals were then inspected to determine which were positively or negatively framed. Any goals with multiple objectives and conflicting frames were organized by only considering the first; for example, "I want to run a marathon and quit smoking" would be considered a positive goal.

With 265 total goals, 184 were positively framed, and 81

were framed negatively. The self-reported success rates were then analyzed to determine the viability of H1. In a ranking from 0-100 (inquiring, "How successful have you been with your objective?"), the majority of participants included a ranking, but those who neglected to were not included in this portion of the assessment. Interestingly, the results confirmed H1, with an average ranking for positive goals at 59.29 versus an average of negative goals at 51.71.

Other collected demographic information included the participant age groups, gender identification, geographic location, and education level completed. While there was a large rate of variability in success rates as a whole, it did not correlate with most of the demographic groups. For instance, there was no discernable pattern of success for any one geographic region versus another. Similarly, there was no perceived pattern of success compared to education level. High school graduates reported roughly the same success rate as participants with advanced degrees. Finally, the success rate related to gender was only somewhat more compelling. There was a higher percentage of females who opted to establish positively framed goals, but the average difference in success rates between genders was negligible.

Survey Two

The second online survey was conducted in February of 2017 to verify the initial findings of the first. The questions were similar, except a few corrected or modified questions (such as correcting the geographic question to ask about the participants' "province" rather than "providence"). Additionally, a few other questions were added. For participants with no goal in mind, "What was the reason (if any) for not making a resolution?" was included. Other new questions surveyed the number of languages spoken by the participants, the number of musical instruments played on a regular basis, and the level of personal optimism about the future. These variables were included to explore a potential link between bilingualism and musicianship with increased self-control (Schroeder, Marian, Shook, & Bartolotti, 2016).

Survey Two featured 403 participants, with 124 who provided goals (roughly the same percentage as the first survey). The initial hypothesis (H1) was evaluated along with two additional conjectures. H2 speculated that the overall success rate would be somewhat lower in Survey Two due to it being conducted a full month after the first survey. H3 speculated that there would be a positive correlation between self-reported success rates and self-reported optimism.

Survey Two supported the initial findings of H1, but only to a limited extent. Of the 124 participants with goals, 84 were positively framed, with an average success rate of 59.61; however, the remaining 40 with negatively framed goals reported an average rate of 58.69. While the positive goals enjoyed higher success as predicted by H1, the difference was marginal. Interestingly, H2 was not confirmed as predicted. The Survey Two data offered average success rates in the 50s, similar to Survey One, counter to the idea that perceived success would decline as time advanced further from the beginning of the New Year. Finally, there was a strong link between the success rates and optimism for H3. Participants with positively framed goals had an average self-reported optimism level of 68.23, while those with negatively framed goals reported optimism of 59.24.

Survey Two found a slightly more compelling difference in success rates and gender than the first survey. The overall success rate for females was 53.57, while the males reported 50.31. Additionally, the overall female optimism level was 66.61, versus the male optimism level of 60.95. However, the results of other demographic groups were less clear. Again, there was no detectable pattern among various age groups, and there was no discernable difference among geographic regions. The difference in success rates by the number of languages spoken and musical instruments was also unclear, partly due the relatively small sample used. Nearly two-thirds of the participants were monolingual, and only about half play one or more instruments regularly. Once these factors are examined in relation to how many also set goals, the sample was too limited to ascertain a reliable inference.

Limitations to the Surveys

Both surveys are inherently limited due to the nature of convenience sampling. It is necessary to sample a finite group of participants to obtain a plausible inference about a larger population (Miah, 2016). While it is not a perfect method, it is not possible to retrieve data from the global population to ascertain undisputable results. However, it is possible to reduce the likelihood of probability errors by using a relatively large sample size (Tversky & Kahneman, 1971).

Accordingly, Survey One had a sample size of 769 total participants, with 265 who reported goals[2]; Survey Two had 403 participants with 124 goal setters[3]. Finally, online surveys are inherently limited due to the necessity of Internet availability and at least moderate computer savviness. While younger computer users are likely more active and comfortable

---

[2] Survey 1 margin of error for goal setters: $1/\sqrt{265} = 6.14\%$
[3] Survey 2 margin of error for goal setters: $1/\sqrt{124} = 8.98\%$

online, older users are presumably less active with Internet usage. Predictably, roughly 73 percent of the combined survey participants were between the ages 18 and 34, leaving much to be desired regarding sampling representativeness (Tversky & Kahneman, 1973).

A Nontraditional Organization

Psychostick, the organization in question, is a musical group that consists of four core members. The band produces a paradoxical style of music that blends two ordinarily separate elements: metal (a stylistic descendant of rock music) and comedy. Additionally, the group formed in 2000 and has developed into a media machine that has released five albums on the record label Rock Ridge Music, dozens of music videos, and has performed over 1,100 shows on two continents (Music, 2017; Videos, 2017; Tour and Events, 2017). The business structure is highly decentralized, with each major business matter agreed upon in a democratic manner. However, each member specializes in several key areas, such as audio engineering, merchandising, Web design, tour management, contract negotiation, and so on.

The group's organizational structure is currently in an unusual state of flux. For many years, the band has operated on an album cycle (write → record → press CDs → sell CDs → tour extensively → repeat). However, the industry in which the band exists is gradually shifting to a new model. There has been a massive transformation from physical album sales to digital purchasing in recent years with global annual music sales dropping from $25.1 billion in 2002 to $15 billion by 2013 (Wikhamn & Knights, 2016). Additionally, over 40 percent of global music and video sales transpire in the U.S. (Music &

Video in the United States, 2015). Curiously, the U.S. music industry reached an all-time high in 2016, with overall music consumption up 3.1 percent since the previous year (Crawford, 2017). While physical CD sales were down 16.3 percent, and digital purchases were down 20.1 percent, on-demand audio streaming enjoyed explosive growth of 76.4 percent (pp. 5-6). Accordingly, a shift from the 1:1 CD transaction model to an audio streaming subscription model is likely imminent. If the preferred method of music consumption is increasingly subscription-based, it would be prudent to adjust accordingly.

Application of Goal Setting Concepts

The band is a compelling example for an organizational case study because there are three distinct operating modes: these include developing and recording songs in the studio, filming music videos, and touring. Recording in a studio environment necessitates a different skill set than filming videos, which in turn is notably dissimilar than performing songs on tour. Accordingly, distinctive goal setting methods may be best implemented depending on the operating mode.

Recording Studio

The band achieved a minor radio hit in 2006 after being picked up by XM Radio (now Sirius XM), eBaum's World, and a collection of regional commercial radio stations around the United States. However, we were fearful of falling into the so-called "sophomore slump," in which bands deliver a poorly received subsequent album following commercial success. The phenomenon is also prevalent in larger organizations, as creativity is often discouraged upon achieving success to exploit the prosperity realized from the previous achievements (Epstein, Kaminaka, Phan, & Uda, 2013). To avert this particular peril, we chose to ignore future external pressures and create whatever seems compelling and enjoyable to us. One might say we chose to adhere to self-set goals rather than succumb to undesirable assigned goals.

There are several ways to help encourage productivity and creativity in the studio. One of the most apparent techniques is to set specific, moderately challenging goals as recommended by goal setting theory. A specific goal might be to complete a song demo by the following Monday to share with the group; a challenging goal might be to compose a musical section of a song with no repeated measures for four straight bars. No repeated melodies for four measures is unconventional due to the nature of rhyming lyrics, which encourages musical repeats to mirror the rhyme scheme. Similarly, there is evidence that this sort of self-regulation can contribute to increased self-efficacy, which in turn encourages greater creativity (Beeftink, Van Eerde, Rutte, & Bertrand, 2012). By cultivating a greater sense of self-efficacy and creative output, it leads to engagement in HPC. With high engagement and artistic fulfillment, each member of the group will, in turn, be committed to perform at increasingly higher levels.

The distinction between performance and mastery goals offers a chance to explore continued musical progress. As any artist would presumably affirm, there is always a new musical style to learn or technique to master. Accordingly, mastery goals may be effective for learning a new way of playing while performance goals may be set once a technique has been mastered. Tracking progress is also important for both forms of goals. For instance, the recording process includes an extensive list of necessary steps to complete a musical work. A given song begins with a demo and scratch vocals; then the arrangement evolves with member input, and each instrumental part must be learned, tracked, mixed, reviewed, and finally mastered[4]. A physical chart may display the extensive list of action items with song titles on the vertical axis and each planned step on the horizontal axis. In fact, this could also lead to an emphasis on sub-goals rather than primary goals to help preserve motivation.

Prospect theory becomes relevant when pursuing goals with so many action items. For instance, it is often more enticing to begin composing a new song than it is to finish a song after working on it for several weeks. The element of diminishing sensitivity to the reference point could promote persistence. As a song nears completion and the chart's boxes are filled up, it could be increasingly exciting and thus motivating to watch it come to fruition. Finally, positive goal framing can induce a challenge response, rather than a threat, within the organization. It could help to keep us galvanized and continually producing celebrated works of art.

Video Production

While songwriting is often initiated independently and semi-complete works are only later brought to the group, filming a music video is often more collaborative. Many of the same strategies from the audio recording process may be adopted, but there are also several unique elements that would be ideal for video production. For instance, organizational creativity is generated by the sum of individual contributions, which

---

[4] There are actually 29 distinct steps taken for each composition, but they have been simplified for readability.

requires high group cohesion (Gupta & Banerjee, 2016). Therefore, it can be helpful to come together to develop story concepts and visual storyboards for video plots.

With the musical element already established, there is less of an issue of metaphorically having too many cooks in the kitchen. Fortunately, the collaborative environment allows members to provide public recognition via positive feedback to team members, which has been shown to be much more motivating than one-on-one recognition (Epstein, Kaminaka, Phan, & Uda, 2013). Finally, it could be a useful exercise to explore each member's sense of IndSC or InterSC regarding personal versus social accomplishments. If the members are relatively outgoing, developing socially-oriented maintenance goals would likely be more effective. Alternatively, more reserved members would likely be motivated more by attainment goals.

Touring

If the processes for audio recording and video production are somewhat similar, the touring life is strikingly divergent. The previous two operational modes exist for the purpose of creating something new while touring offers a chance to perform for music listeners in far-reaching geographical regions. However, the logistics of touring across the nation or multiple countries requires months of preparation which includes promotion, ordering merchandise, obtaining visas, and many other action items[5]. With such an expansive list of responsibilities to enjoy a successful and prosperous tour, it

---

[5] Similar to the necessary steps to record a song, touring requires numerous action items; however, the specific requirements differ depending on the scope, destination, and duration of the tour.

requires that all members possess a great deal of intrinsic motivation. Fortunately, high intrinsic motivation is also a predictor of individual creativity and increases the personal perception of enjoyment of a given task (Hannam & Narayan, 2015). Motivated individuals tend to view difficult tasks as an opportunity to accomplish important achievements rather than as a burden.

If motivation is such an important element to the enjoyment of a task, and thus, persistence, it is vital to consider how to increase intrinsic motivation. Maintaining a focus on sub-goals can help to retain motivation by reducing the overwhelming sense of juggling dozens of responsibilities each day. These sub-goals could be anything from arriving at the venue by the established load-in time to collecting the guarantee (the industry term for the pre-determined fee paid to bands), to selling a certain amount of merchandise each night.

Personal goals should be aligned with group goals to ensure there is not a significant conflict. The stereotypical band member who perpetually wishes to be home with his or her significant other should not be on the road if the group hopes to preserve a modicum of morale. Finally, hedonic adaptation may be employed by balancing each operational mode and not strictly recording for months at a time or touring for months without reprieve. Shorter tours, perhaps limited to about three weeks, can be scheduled to maximize enjoyment and perhaps even mental well-being. Finishing a tour in an exceptional market can also help each member to remember the entire excursion more fondly. Affectionately recalling tours can mean the difference between perceiving one as a collective success or an abysmal failure.

Personal Takeaways

I have had the supreme pleasure to perform with my band in 48 states, three Canadian provinces, as well as cities in England, Scotland, and Wales in recent years. Additionally, I have established other personal targets including the pursuit of several academic degrees and professional certifications. To simultaneously accomplish these goals I have had to develop effective ways in which to establish, pursue, and persist in completing my goals consistently. Accordingly, goal setting is an especially meaningful personal motif.

While goal setting theory is quite compelling, I am particularly interested in various personal quirks revealed by behavioral economics. Adapting prospect theory, hedonic adaptation, and framing to the realm of goal setting was, therefore, a fascinating process. Rather than strictly point out anticipated flaws of consistency, I was able to adapt goal setting to the common strengths shared by most people to help improve personal habits. The goal framing survey results were equally intriguing. It was quite satisfying to obtain results that agreed with my hypotheses and just as interesting to learn where my presumptions were somewhat erroneous.

Finally, the goal setting recommendations are not limited to graduate students with outrageous schedules and professional responsibilities perpetually competing for time. Many of these goal setting concepts may apply to individuals in all sorts of circumstances, as well as organizations with diverse backgrounds. Achieving challenging goals requires direct effort and can help to improve decision making to attain greater outcomes.

Conclusion

Goal setting is a comprehensive way for individuals and organizations to accomplish ambitious tasks. It may be as simple as answering a trivia question correctly or as perplexing as developing a theory of human consciousness. Goal setting theory makes several suggestions to help accomplish greater feats, such as to set high, moderately challenging goals. Behavioral economics offers an unusual perspective by pointing out potential pitfalls in human action and reasoning. One human quirk is known as framing, which was tested with survey participants who set goals. Finally, many of the concepts discussed were theoretically applied to the author's organization to help its members establish superior goals to enjoy exceptional results.

References

Amir, O., & Ariely, D. (2008). Resting on laurels: The effects of discrete progress markers as subgoals on task performance and preferences. *Journal of Experimental Psychology: Learning, Memory, and Cognition, 34*(5), 1158–1171. doi:10.1037/a0012857

Ariely, D. (1998). Combining experiences over time: The effects of duration, intensity changes and on-line measurements on retrospective pain evaluations. *Journal of Behavioral Decision Making, 11*(1), 19-45. doi:10.1002/(SICI) 1099-0771(199803)11:1<19::AID-BDM277>3.0.CO;2-B

Bandura, A., & Locke, E. A. (2003). Negative self-efficacy and goal effects revisited. *Journal of Applied Psychology, 88*(1), 87-99. doi:10.1037/0021-9010.88.1.87

Beeftink, F., Van Eerde, W., Rutte, C. G., & Bertrand, J. W. M. (2012). Being successful in a creative profession: The role of innovative cognitive style, self-regulation, and self-efficacy. *Journal of Business & Psychology, 27*(1), 71-81. doi:10.1007/s10869-011-9214-9

Berns, G., Laibson, D. and Loewenstein, G. (2007). Intertemporal choice: Toward an integrative framework. *Trends in Cognitive Sciences, 11*(11), 482-488. doi:10.1016/J.TICS.2007.08.011

Brickman, P., Coates, D., & Janoff-Bulman, R. (1978). Lottery winners and accident victims: Is happiness relative? *Journal of Personality and Social Psychology, 36*(8), 917-927. doi:10.1037/0022-3514.36.8.917

Christakis, N. A., & Fowler, J. H. (2007). The spread of obesity in a large social network over 32 years. *New England Journal of Medicine, 357*(4), 370-379. doi:10.1056/NEJMsa066082

Crawford, E. (2017). Nielsen music year-end report U.S. 2016. *Nielsen.* Retrieved from http://www.nielsen.com/us/en/insights/reports/2017/ 2016-music-us-year-end-report.html

Cross, S. E., Hardin, E. E., & Gercek-Swing, B. (2011). The what, how, why, and where of self-construal. *Personality and Social Psychology Review, 15*(2) 142–179. doi:10.1177/1088868310373752

Drach- Zahavya, A., & Erez, M. (2002). Challenge versus threat effects on the goal–performance relationship. *Organizational Behavior and Human Decision Processes 88*(2), 667–682. doi:10.1016/S0749-5978(02)00004-3

Elliot, A. J., & Church, M. A. (1997). A hierarchical model of approach and avoidance achievement motivation. *Journal of Personality and Social Psychology, 72*(1), 218-232. doi:10.1037/0022-3514.72.1.218

Elliot, A. J., & Fryer, J. W. (2008). The goal construct in psychology. *Handbook of Motivation Science, 18*, 235–250.

Elliot, A. J., & Harackiewicz, J. M. (1996). Approach and avoidance achievement goals and intrinsic motivation: A mediational analysis. *Journal of Personality and Social Psychology, 70*(3), 461-475. doi:10.1037/0022-3514.70.3.461

Epstein, R., Kaminaka, K., Phan, V., & Uda, R. (2013). How is creativity best managed? Some empirical and theoretical guidelines. *Creativity & Innovation Management, 22*(4), 359-374. doi:10.1111/caim.12042

Foss, N. J., & Lindenberg, S. (2013). Microfoundations for strategy: A goal-framing perspective on the drivers of value creation. *Academy of Management Perspectives, 27*(2), 85-102. doi:10.5465/amp.2012.0103

Frederick, S., & Loewenstein, G. (1999). Hedonic adaptation. In *Well-being: The foundations of hedonic psychology.* Kahneman, D., Diener, E., & Schwarz, N. (Eds.). (pp. 302-329). New York, NY: Russell Sage Foundation Press.

Gagnon-Girouard, M., Begin, C., Provencher, V., Tremblay, A., Mongeau, L., Boivin, S., & Lemieux, S. (2010). Psychological impact of a "health-at-every-size" intervention on weight-preoccupied overweight/obese women. *Journal of Obesity, 2010*, 1-12. doi:10.1155/2010/928097

Gupta, R., & Banerjee, P. (2016). Antecedents of organisational creativity: A multi-level approach. *Business: Theory & Practice, 17*(2), 167-177. doi:10.3846/btp.2016.624

Hannam, K., & Narayan, A. (2015). Intrinsic motivation, organizational justice, and creativity. *Creativity Research Journal, 27*(2), 214-224. doi:10.1080/10400419.2015.1030307

Heath, C., Larrick, R. P., & Wu, G. (1999). Goals as reference points. *Cognitive Psychology 38*(1), 79–109. doi:10.1006/cogp.1998.0708

Houser-Marko, L., & Sheldon, K. M. (2008). Eyes on the prize or nose to the grindstone? The effects of level of goal evaluation on mood and motivation. *Personality and Social Psychology Bulletin, 34*(11), 1556-1569. doi:10.1177/0146167208322618

Ji Hoon, J., & Lynch Jr., J. G. (2015). Pardon the interruption: Goal proximity, perceived spare time, and impatience. *Journal of Consumer Research, 41*(5), 1267-1283. doi:10.1086/679308

Kahneman, D., & Tversky, A. (1979). Prospect theory: An analysis of decision under risk. *Econometrica, 47*(2), 263-292. doi:10.2307/1914185

Kahneman, D., & Tversky, A. (1984). Choices, values, and frames. *American Psychologist, 39*(4), 341-350. doi:10.1037/0003-066X.39.4.341

Latham, G. P., & Locke, E. A. (2007). New developments in and directions for goal setting research. *European Psychologist, 12*(4), 290-300. doi:10.1027/1016-9040.12.4.290

Latham, G. P., & Piccolo, R. F. (2012). The effect of context-specific versus nonspecific subconscious goals on employee performance. *Human Resource Management, 51*(4), 511-523. doi:10.1002/hrm.21486

Latham, G. P., & Pinder, C. C. (2005). Work motivation theory and research at the dawn of the Twenty-First Century. *Annual Review of Psychology, 56*, 485-516. doi:10.1146/annurev.psych.55.090902.142105

Latham, G. P., Stajkovic, A. D., & Locke, E. A. (2010). The relevance and viability of subconscious goals in the workplace. *Journal of Management, 36*(1), 234-255. doi:10.1177/0149206309350777

Locke, E. A., & Latham, G. P. (2002). Building a practically useful theory of goal setting and task motivation: A 35-year odyssey. *American Psychologist, 57*(9), 705–717. doi:10.1037//0003-066X.57.9.705

Locke, E. A., & Latham, G. P. (2006). New directions in goal-setting theory. *Current Directions in Psychological Science, 15*(5), 265-268. doi:10.1111/j.1467-8721.2006.00449.x

Locke, E. A., Shaw, K. N., Saari, L. M., & Latham, G. P. (1981). Goal setting and task performance: 1969-1980. *Psychological Bulletin, 90*(1), 125-152. doi:10.1037/0033-2909.90.1.125

Miah, A. Q. (2016). *Applied statistics for social and management sciences.* Singapore: Springer. doi:10.1007/978-981-10-0401-8

Mochon, D., Norton, M. I., & Ariely, D. (2008). Getting off the hedonic treadmill, one step at a time: The impact of regular religious practice and exercise on well-being. *Journal of Economic Psychology, 29*(5), 632–642. doi:10.1016/j.joep.2007.10.004

Music. (2017). *Psychostick.* Retrieved from http://psychostick.com/music

Music & Video in the United States. (2015). Music & video industry profile: United States. *Marketline*, 1-38.

Nutrition Facts. (2009). Chocolate tower truffle cake. *The Cheesecake Factory.* Retrieved from http://www.cheesecakefactorynutrition.com/restaurant-item.php?rid=58&mid=2247?

Ogden, C. L., Carroll, M. D., Fryar, C. D., & Flegal, K. M. (2015). Prevalence of obesity among adults and youth: United States, 2011–2014. *Centers for Disease Control and Prevention, 219*, 1-7. Retrieved from https://www.cdc.gov/nchs/data/databriefs/db219.pdf

Paulson, S., Albert, D., Holt, J., & Turok, N. (2015). The origins of the Universe: Why is there something rather than nothing?. *Annals of the New York Academy of Sciences, 1361*(1), 1-17. doi:10.1111/nyas.12859

Polivy, J., Coleman, J., & Herman, C. P. (2005). The effect of deprivation on food cravings and eating behavior in restrained and unrestrained eaters. *International Journal of Eating Disorders, 38*(4), 301-309. doi:10.1002/EAT.20195

Provencher, V., Begin, C., Tremblay, A., Mongeau, L., Corneau, L., Dodin, S., Boivin, S., & Lemieux, S. (2009). Health-at-every-size and eating behaviors: 1-year follow-up results of a size acceptance intervention. *Journal of the American Dietetic Association, 109*(11), 1854-1861. doi:10.1016/J.JADA.2009.08.017

Rawsthorne, L. J., & Elliot, A. J. (1999). Achievement goals and intrinsic motivation: A meta-analytic review. *Personality & Social Psychology Review, 3*(4), 326-344. doi:10.1207/s15327957pspr0304_3

Roney, C. R., & Lehman, D. R. (2008). Self-regulation in goal striving: Individual differences and situational moderators of the goal-framing/performance link. *Journal of Applied Social Psychology, 38*(11), 2691-2709. doi:10.1111/j.1559-1816.2008.00410.x

Schroeder, S. R., Marian, V., Shook, A., & Bartolotti, J. (2016). Bilingualism and musicianship enhance cognitive control. *Neural Plasticity*, 1-11. doi:10.1155/2016/4058620

Seijts, G. H., & Latham, G. P. (2005). Learning versus performance goals: When should each be used?. *Academy of Management Executive, 19*(1), 124-131. doi:10.5465/AME.2005.15841964

Sun, R. (2009). Motivational representations within a computational cognitive architecture. *Cognitive Computation, 1*(1), 91–103. doi:10.1007/s12559-009-9005-z

Thaler, R. H. (2016). Behavioral economics: Past, present, and future. *American Economic Review, 106*(7), 1577-1600. doi:10.1257/aer.106.7.1577

Thaler, R. H., & Sunstein, C. H. (2008). *Nudge: Improving decisions about health, wealth, and happiness*. New Haven, CT: Yale University Press.

Tour and Events. (2017). Past shows. *Psychostick*. Retrieved from http://psychostick.com/tour?past=eatfecesharhar

Tversky, A., & Kahneman, D. (1971). Belief in the law of small numbers. *Psychological Bulletin, 76*(2), 105-110. doi:10.1037/h0031322

Tversky, A., & Kahneman, D. (1973). Availability: A heuristic for judging frequency and probability. *Cognitive Psychology, 5*(2), 207-232. doi:10.1016/0010-0285(73)90033-9

Videos. (2017). Videos, page 1. *Psychostick*. Retrieved from http://psychostick.com/videos

Wikhamn, B. R., & Knights, D. (2016). Associations for disruptiveness: The Pirate Bay vs. Spotify. *Journal of Technology Management & Innovation, 11*(3), 40-49. doi:10.4067/S0718-27242016000300005

Yang, H., Stamatogiannakis, A., & Chattopadhyay, A. (2015). Pursuing attainment versus maintenance goals: The interplay of self-construal and goal type on consumer motivation. *Journal of Consumer Research, 42*(1), 93-108. doi:10.1093/jcr/ucv008

Zauberman, G., Diehl, K., & Ariely, D. (2006). Hedonic versus informational evaluations: Task dependent preferences for sequences of outcomes. *Journal of Behavioral Decision Making, 19*(3), 191-211. doi:10.1002/bdm.516

APPENDIX C: LIST OF CLASSES

2011

DEV 031 - Pre-Algebra

FMGT 101 - Personal Finance

2012

ACCT 106 - Financial Accounting

FMGT 211 - Investments

MATH 102 - Beginning Algebra I

ACCT 107 - Managerial Accounting

ENGL 111 - English Composition

MATH 103 - Beginning Algebra II

CIT 101 - PC Applications

ECON 200 - Principles of Microeconomics

FMGT 201 - Corporate Finance

BMGT 1111 - Management

BOA 1200 - Business Language

ECON 2201 - Principles of Macroeconomics

2013

FMGT 2242 - International Finance

LEGL 2064 - Legal Environment of Business

MKTG 1110 - Marketing Principles

PSY 1100 - Introduction to Psychology

BOA 1300 - Business Applications

FMGT 2202 - Money & Banking

STAT 1350 - Elementary Statistics

BMGT 2216 - Business Ethics

MATH 1075 - Intermediate Algebra

PHIL 1101 - Introduction to Philosophy

2014

ASTR 1162 - Stars and Galaxies

BMGT 2299 - Case Study Strategic Management

FMGT 2299 - Finance Capstone

Associate of Applied Science in Finance

PF 321 - Learning Strategies

COMM 1105 - Interpersonal Communication

SOC 1101 - Introduction to Sociology

HUMN 305 - Global Issues

ECON 322 - Intermediate Macroeconomics

FPLN 430 - Income Tax Planning

2015

FINA 403 - Advanced Financial Management

FPLN 440 - Insurance Planning

FPLN 450 - Retirement Planning

FPLN 460 - Estate Planning

BIO 1112 - Human Biology

PHIL 1130 - Ethics

FINA 495 - Financial Policy Seminar

FPLN 495 - Financial Planning Seminar

2016

HUMN 210 - Intro to Logic & Critical Thinking Skills

PSYC 601 - Introduction to Business Psychology

PSYC 602 - Individual & Organizational Intelligence

Bachelor of Science in Financial Planning & Financial Management

PSYC 603 - Managerial Psychology

PSYC 604 - Behavioral Economics & Neurofinance

PSYC 605 - Psychology of Marketing

PSYC 606 - Psychology of Human Resources

PSYC 607 - Psychology of Creativity, Innovation, & Change

2017

PSYC 608 - Psychology of Organizational Coaching

PSYC 609 - Business Psychology Mastery Demonstration

Master of Science in Business Psychology

REFERENCES

INTRODUCTION TO TOUR LIFE

Tour and Events. (2019). *Psychostick*. http://psychostick.com/tour

Countries That Use Imperial 2019. (2019). *World Population Review*. http://worldpopulationreview.com/countries/ countries-that-use-imperial

CHAPTER 2011

Academic Testing. (2018). College testing services. *Columbus State Community College*. https://www.cscc.edu/services/ testingcenter/academic-testing/index.shtml

Testing Centers. (2019). Testing. *Metropolitan Community Colleges*. https://mcckc.edu/testing

Keown, A. J. (2015). *Personal finance: Turning money into wealth* (7th ed.). Pearson.

Ariely, D., & Kreisler, J. (2017). *Dollars and sense: How we misthink money and how to spend smarter*. HarperCollins Publishers.

Duffin, E. (2019). United States: Inflation rate from 1990 to 2019. *Statista*. https://www.statista.com/statistics/ 191077/inflation-rate-in-the-usa-since-1990

Akerlof, G. A., & Shiller, R. J. (2009). *Animal spirits: How human psychology drives the economy, and why it matters for global capitalism*. Princeton University Press.

Graham, B. (2006). *The intelligent investor: The definitive book on value investing* (Revised ed.). HarperCollins Publishers.

CHAPTER 2012

Testing Center. (2019). The Park University Testing Center. *Park University*. https://www.park.edu/academics/academic-support-center/testing-center

Isaacson, W. (2007). *Einstein: His life and universe.* Simon & Schuster.

Testing Services. (2019). Academics. *Moraine Valley Community College.* https://www.morainevalley.edu/academics/testing-services

Tversky, A., & Kahneman, D. (1974). Judgment under uncertainty: Heuristics and biases. *Science* (New Series), 185, 1124-1131.

United States Population 2019. (2019). *World Population Review.* http://worldpopulationreview.com/countries/united-states-population

US States - Ranked by Population 2019. (2019). *World Population Review.* http://worldpopulationreview.com/states

Murphy, C. B. (2019). Financial statements. *Investopedia.* https://www.investopedia.com/terms/f/financial-statements.asp

Ross, S. (2019). How financial accounting differs from managerial accounting. *Investopedia.* https://www.investopedia.com/ask/answers041015/how-does-financial-accounting-differ-managerial-accounting.asp

IFPI Global Music Report 2019. (2019). *IFPI.* https://ifpi.org/news/IFPI-GLOBAL-MUSIC-REPORT-2019

Testing Centers & Labs. (2019). Academics. *Laramie County Community College.* http://lccc.wy.edu/academics/services/examLab/index.aspx

Testing Services. (n.d.). Student life. *University of Montana.* https://www.umt.edu/testing/

Testing Center. (2019). Current students. *Odessa College.* https://www.odessa.edu/current-students/testing/

Finance AAS. (2018). Finance. *Columbus State Community College.* https://www.cscc.edu/academics/departments/finance/

Mankiw, N. G. (2014). *Principles of microeconomics* (7th ed.). Cengage Learning.

Brealey, R., Myers, S., & Marcus, A. (2019). *Fundamentals of corporate finance* (12th ed.). McGraw-Hill Education.

Kahneman, D. (2011). *Thinking, fast and slow*. Farrar, Straus and Giroux.

CHAPTER 2013

Testing Center. (2019). *Community College of Denver.* https://www.ccd.edu/org/testing-center

University Testing Center. (n.d.). Student development and enrollment services. *University of Central Florida.* https://utc.sdes.ucf.edu

Myers, D. G., & DeWall, C. N. (2017). *Psychology* (12th ed.). Worth Publishers.

Allen, C. P. G., Sumner, P., & Chambers, C. D. (2014). The timing and neuroanatomy of conscious vision as revealed by TMS-induced blindsight. *Journal of Cognitive Neuroscience, 26*(7), 1507-1518. https://doi.org/10.1162/jocn_a_00557

Wang, R. (2013). Heavy metal drummer uses online college scholarship to earn finance degree. *GetEducated.* https://www.geteducated.com/free-college-scholarships/537-heavy-metal-drummer-uses-online-college-scholarship-to-earn-finance-degree

Blastland, M. (2010). *The numbers game: The commonsense guide to understanding numbers in the news, in politics, and in life.* Avery Publishing Group.

Grumman Lunar Module LM-13. (2019). Exploring space. *Cradle of Aviation Museum.* https://www.cradleofaviation.org/ history/exhibits/exhibit-galleries/exploring_space/grumman_ lunar_module_lm-13.html

NASA Facts. (2004). Benefits from Apollo: Giant leaps in technology. *National Aeronautics and Space Administration.* https://www.nasa.gov/sites/default/ files/80660main_ ApolloFS.pdf

Distance Testing Center. (n.d.). Placement Testing. *Nassau Community College.* https://www.ncc.edu/ placementtesting/distance_testing _services.shtml

Candy Crush Saga. (2019). Games. *King.* https://king.com/game/candycrush

Bowers, M. (2013). Words with math. *TEDxColumbus.* https://www.youtube.com/watch?v=WVVBVgBOp9M

Friedman, M., Mackey, J., & Rodger, T. J. (2005). Rethinking the social responsibility of business. *Reason.* https://reason.com/2005/10/01/rethinking-the-social-responsi-2

Mackey, J. & Sisodia, R. (2014). *Conscious capitalism: Liberating the heroic spirit of business.* Harvard Business Review Press.

CHAPTER 2014

Buffett, W. (1997). Chairman's letter. *Berkshire Hathaway.* https://www.berkshirehathaway.com/1996ar/1996.html

2012 Annual Report. (2013). *Bristol-Myers Squibb.* http://www.annualreports.com/HostedData/AnnualReportArchive/b/NYSE_BMY_2012.pdf

Buffett, W. (2003). Annual report. *Berkshire Hathaway.* https://www.berkshirehathaway.com/letters/2002pdf.pdf

Lewis, M. (2010). *The big short: Inside the doomsday machine.* Norton and Company.

Hawking, S. (2001). *The Universe in a nutshell.* Bantam Dell.

Commencement Ceremonies. (2014). *Columbus State Community College.* https://www.cscc.edu/services/graduation/pdf/GraduationProgram.MAY.2014.pdf

Preferred Pathway. (2018). Transfer partnerships. *Columbus State Community College.* https://www.cscc.edu/academics/transfer/preferred-pathway

Hoffman, J. M., Creevy, K. E., & Promislow, D. E. L. (2013). Reproductive capability is associated with lifespan and cause of death in companion dogs. *PLoS ONE, 8*(4), e61082. https://doi.org/10.1371/journal.pone.0061082

State of Pet Health 2013 Report. (2013). *Banfield Pet Hospital.* https://www.banfield.com/Banfield/media/PDF/Downloads/soph/Banfield-State-of-Pet-Health-Report_2013.pdf

Pariona, A. (2017). What language do they speak in Romania? *World Atlas.* https://www.worldatlas.com/ articles/what-language-do-they-speak-in-romania.html

Sen Nag, O. (2017). What languages are spoken in Moldova? *World Atlas.* https://www.worldatlas.com/articles/what-languages-are-spoken-in-moldova.html

Mallonee, L. (2016). Meet the people of a Soviet country that doesn't exist. *Wired.* https://www.wired.com/2016/03/meet-people-transnistria-stuck-time-soviet-country-doesnt-exist

Country Overview. (n.d.). The Pridnestrovien Moldavian Republic. *Ministry of Foreign Affairs of Pridnestrovien Moldavian Republic.* http://mfa-pmr.org/en/KGR

Challa, J. (2013). Why being 'gypped' hurts the Roma more than it hurts you. *NPR.* https://www.npr.org/sections/codeswitch/2013/12/30/242429836/why-being-gypped-hurts-the-roma-more-than-it-hurts-you

Exam Readiness Guide. (2019). Franklin University. *ProctorU.* https://www.proctoru.com/portal/franklin

CHAPTER 2015

Musk, E. (2014). All our patent are belong to you. *Tesla.* https://www.tesla.com/en_CA/blog/all-our-patent-are-belong-you

Nye, B. (2014). *Undeniable: Evolution and the science of creation.* St. Martin's Press.

Nye, B. (2015). *Unstoppable: Harnessing science to change the world.* St. Martin's Press.

Cook, J., Oreskes, N., Doran, P. T. Anderegg, W. R. L., Verheggen, B., Maibach, E. W., Carlton, J. S., Lewandowsky, S., Skuce, A. G., Green, S. A., Nuccitelli, D., Jacobs, P., Richardson, M., Winkler, B., Painting, R., & Rice, K. (2016). Consensus on consensus: A synthesis of consensus estimates on human-caused global warming. *Environmental Research Letters, 11*, 048002. https://doi.org/:10.1088/1748-9326/11/4/048002

Oreskes, N., & Conway, E. M. (2010). *Merchants of doubt: How a handful of scientists obscured the truth on issues from tobacco smoke to global warming.* Bloomsbury Press.

Edelman, G. M. (2005). *Wider than the sky: The phenomenal gift of consciousness.* Yale University Press.

Strauch, B. (2010). *The secret life of the grown-up brain: The surprising talents of the middle-aged mind.* Penguin Books.

Gerdts, V., van Drunen Littel-van den Hurk, S., Griebel, P. J., & Babiuk, L. A. (2007). Use of animal models in the development of human vaccines. *Future Microbiology, 2*(6), 667-675. https://doi.org/10.2217/17460913.2.6.667

PHS Policy on Humane Care and Use of Laboratory Animals. (2015). Policies and laws. *NIH Office of Laboratory Animal Welfare.* https://olaw.nih.gov/policies-laws/phs-policy.htm

Rachels, J., & Rachels, S. (2012). *The elements of moral philosophy* (7th ed.). McGraw-Hill Learning Solutions.

Newest Members at Franklin University. (2015). *Sigma Beta Delta.* https://sigmabetadelta.org/newest-members-franklin-university

CHAPTER 2016

Super MAGFest. (2019). *MAGFest.* https://super.magfest.org

Ratcliff, R., Smith, P. L., Brown, S. D., & McKoon, G. (2017). Diffusion decision model: Current issues and history. *Trends in Cognitive Sciences, 20*(4), 260-281. https://doi.org/10.1016/j.tics.2016.01.007

Platon, A. (2016). B.o.B tries to convince Twitter Earth is flat, Neil deGrasse Tyson responds. *Billboard.* https://www.billboard.com/articles/columns/hip-hop/6851778/bob-earth-flat-twitter-neil-degrasse-tyson

Pogge, R. W. (2017). Real-world relativity: The GPS navigation system. *Ohio State University.* http://www.astronomy.ohio-state.edu/~pogge/Ast162/Unit5/gps.html

Herculano-Houzel, S. (2016). *The human advantage: A new understanding of how our brain became remarkable.* MIT Press.

Forbes, R. L., Jones, B., & Jones, K. (2014). Business psychology: Building an interdisciplinary bridge from the ground up. *American International Journal of Social Science, 3(*2), 10-17.

Horstman, J. (2010). *The scientific American: Brave new brain.* San Jossey-Bass.

Ariely, D., & Berns, G. (2010). Neuromarketing: The hope and hype of neuroimaging in business. *Nature Reviews Neuroscience, 11*(4), 284-292. https://doi.org/10.1038/nrn2795

Burgess, R. (2011). MEG: Magnetoencephalography. *Cleveland Clinic: Neurological Institute.* http://my.clevelandclinic.org/ccf/media/Files/Epilepsy_Center/MEG-2011.pdf

Öisjöen, F., Schneiderman, J. F., Figueras, G. A., Chukharkin, M. L., Kalabukhov, A., Hedström, A., Elam, M., & Winkler, D. (2012). High-Tc superconducting quantum interference device recordings of spontaneous brain activity: Towards high-Tc magnetoencephalography. *Applied Physics Letters, 100*(13), 1-4. https://doi.org/10.1063/1.3698152

Benyus, J. (2009). Biomimicry in action. *TEDGlobal 2009.* http://www.ted.com/talks/janine_benyus_biomimicry_in_action

Levinson, H. (1973). Asinine attitudes toward motivation. *Harvard Business Review, 51*(1), 70-76.

Forbes, R. L., Igonor, A., & Kuehnl, K. F. (2017). Biology, business and brain science: The strangest of attractors? *Advances in Social Sciences Research Journal, 4(*14) 71-83.

Kirschner P. A., & De Bruyckere, P. (2017). The myths of the digital native and the multitasker. *Teaching and Teacher Education, 67*, 135-142. https://doi.org/10.1016/j.tate.2017.06.001

Ariely, D. (2009). *Predictably irrational: The hidden forces that shape our decisions* (2nd ed.). HarperCollins Publishers.

Ariely, D. (2010). *The upside of irrationality: The unexpected benefits of defying logic.* HarperCollins Publishers.

Ariely, D. (2012). *The (honest) truth about dishonesty: How we lie to everyone—especially ourselves.* HarperCollins Publishers.

Day, M., & Gu, J. (2019). The enormous numbers behind Amazon's market reach. *Bloomberg.* https://www.bloomberg.com/graphics/2019-amazon-reach-across-markets

Barden, P. (2013). *Decoded: The science behind why we buy.* John Wiley & Sons.

Gold, J. I., & Heekeren, H. R. (2014). Neural mechanisms for perceptual decision making. In P. W. Glimcher, & E. Fehr (Eds.). *Neuroeconomics: Decision making and the brain* (2nd ed.), (pp. 355-372). Academic Press.

Chamberlin, J. (2009). Overgeneralizing the generations. *Monitor on Psychology, 40*(6), 40.

Conover, A. (2016). Millennials don't exist! Adam Conover on Deep Shift. *Adam Conover.* https://www.youtube.com/watch?v=-HFwok9SlQQ

Trzesniewski, K. H., & Donnellan, M. B. (2010). Rethinking "Generation Me": A study of cohort effects from 1976–2006. *Perspectives on Psychological Science, 5*(1) 58–75. https://doi.org/10.1177/1745691609356789

Rock, D. (2009). *Your brain at work: Strategies for overcoming distraction, regaining focus, and working smarter all day long.* HarperCollins Publishers.

Nussbaum, B. (2013). *Creative intelligence: Harnessing the power to create, connect, and inspire.* Harper Business.

CHAPTER 2017

Roney, C. R., & Lehman, D. R. (2008). Self-regulation in goal striving: Individual differences and situational moderators of the goal-framing/performance link. *Journal of Applied Social Psychology, 38*(11), 2691–2709. https://doi.org/10.1111/j.1559-1816.2008. 00410.x

Locke, E. A., & Latham, G. P. (2002). Building a practically useful theory of goal setting and task motivation: A 35-year odyssey. *American Psychologist, 57*(9), 705-717. https://doi.org/10.1037//0003-066X.57.9.705

Deck of Cards. (2017). Deck of cards official music video. *Ideamen.* https://www.youtube.com/watch?v=A1BFdTJ1fr0

Houser-Marko, L., & Sheldon, K. M. (2008). Eyes on the prize or nose to the grindstone? The effects of level of goal evaluation on mood and motivation. *Personality and Social Psychology Bulletin, 34*(11), 1556-1569. https://doi.org/10.1177/0146167208322618

Ariely, D. (2010). *The upside of irrationality: The unexpected benefits of defying logic.* HarperCollins Publishers.

Brickman, P., Coates, D., & Janoff-Bulman, R. (1978). Lottery winners and accident victims: Is happiness relative? *Journal of Personality and Social Psychology, 36*(8), 917-927. https://doi.org/10.1037/0022-3514.36.8.917

Cuddy, A. (2015). *Presence: Bringing your boldest self to your biggest challenges.* Little, Brown & Company.

TO BE CONTINUED

Scarpelli, L. (2015). Goodbye, music Tuesday: Starting today, albums come out on Friday. *NPR.* https://www.npr.org/sections/therecord/2015/07/10/421483599/goodbye-music-tuesday-starting-today-albums-come-out-on-Friday

Loewenstein, G. (2005). Hot-cold empathy gaps and medical decision-making. *Health Psychology, 24*(4), S49-S56. https://doi.org/10.1037/0278-6133.24.4.S49

Ariely, D., & Loewenstein, G. (2006). The heat of the moment: The effect of sexual arousal on sexual decision making. *Journal of Behavioral Decision Making, 19*(2), 87-98. https://doi.org/10.1002/bdm.501

INDEX

RECOMMENDED READING

Interesting and inspiring books that have helped me persevere

Akerlof, G. A., & Shiller, R. J. (2009). *Animal spirits: How human psychology drives the economy, and why it matters for global capitalism.* Princeton University Press.

Alter, A. (2017). *Irresistible: The rise of addictive technology and the business of keeping us hooked.* Penguin Press.

Arden, J. (2014). *The brain bible: A plan to stay vital, productive, and happy for a lifetime.* McGraw-Hill Education.

Ariely, D. (2009). *Predictably irrational: The hidden forces that shape our decisions* (2nd ed.). HarperCollins Publishers.

Ariely, D. (2010). *The upside of irrationality: The unexpected benefits of defying logic.* HarperCollins Publishers.

Ariely, D. (2016). *Payoff: The hidden logic that shapes our motivations.* TED Books.

Ariely, D., & Kreisler, J. (2017). *Dollars and sense: How we misthink money and how to spend smarter.* HarperCollins Publishers.

Avalon, M. (2001). *Secrets of negotiating a record contract: The musician's guide to understanding and avoiding sneaky lawyer tricks.* Backbeat Books.

Avalon, M. (2016). *Confessions of a record producer: How to survive the scams and shams of the music business* (5th ed.). Backbeat Books.

Barden, P. (2013). *Decoded: The science behind why we buy.* John Wiley & Sons.

Barker, T., & Edwards, G. (2015). *Can I say: Living large, cheating death, and drums, drums, drums.* HarperCollins Publishers.

Baumeister, R. F., & Tierney, J. (2012). *Willpower: Rediscovering the greatest human strength* (Reprint ed.). Penguin Books.

Bogle, J. C. (2012). *Investment vs. speculation: The clash of the cultures.* John Wiley & Sons.

Cain, S. (2013). *Quiet: The power of introverts in a world that can't stop talking.* Random House.

Carr, N. (2011). *The shallows: What the Internet is doing to our brains.* W. W. Norton & Company.

Costandi, M. (2016). *Neuroplasticity.* The MIT Press.

Cuddy, A. (2015). *Presence: Bringing your boldest self to your biggest challenges.* Little, Brown & Company.

Dessa. (2018). *My own devices: Essays from the road on music, science, and senseless love.* E. P. Dutton.

Doidge, N. (2007). *The brain that changes itself: Stories of personal triumph from the frontiers of brain science.* Penguin Books.

Doidge, N. (2015). *The brain's way of healing: Remarkable discoveries and recoveries from the frontiers of neuroplasticity.* Penguin Books.

Duckworth, A. (2016). *Grit: The power of passion and perseverance.* Scribner.

Dweck, C. S. (2007). *Mindset: The new psychology of success* (Updated ed.). Ballantine Books.

Edelman, G. M. (2005). *Wider than the sky: The phenomenal gift of consciousness.* Yale University Press.

Eriksson, M. E. (2019). *Another primordial day: The paleo metal diaries.* PMET Publishing House.

Gazzaley, A., & Rozen, L. D. (2016). *The distracted mind: Ancient brains in a high-tech world.* MIT Press.

Gazzaniga, M. (2015). *Tales from both sides of the brain: A life in neuroscience.* Ecco.

Gilovich, T., & Ross, L. (2015). *The wisest one in the room: How you can benefit from social psychology's most powerful insights.* Free Press.

Godfrey-Smith, P. (2016). *Other minds: The octopus, the sea, and the deep origins of consciousness.* Farrar, Straus, & Giroux.

Graham, B. (2006). *The intelligent investor: The definitive book on value investing* (Revised ed.). HarperCollins Publishers.

Grant, A. (2016). *Originals: How non-conformists move the world.* Viking Books.

Harari, Y. N. (2014). *Sapiens: A brief history of humankind.* Harper Perennial.

Harari, Y. N. (2017). *Homo deus: A brief history of tomorrow.* Signal Books.

Hawking, S. (1996). *The illustrated a brief history of time.* Bantam Dell.

Hawking, S. (2001). *The universe in a nutshell.* Bantam Dell.

Hawking, S. (2013). *My brief history.* Bantam Books.

Hawking, S., & Mlodinow, L. (2010). *The grand design.* Bantam Dell.

Hawkins, J., & Blakeslee, S. (2004). *On intelligence: How a new understanding of the brain will lead to the creation of truly intelligent machines.* Times Books.

Heath, C., & Heath, D. (2010). *Switch: How to change things when change is hard.* Broadway Books.

Heath, C., & Heath, D. (2013). *Decisive: How to make better choices in life and work.* Crown Business.

Heath, C., & Heath, D. (2017). *The power of moments: Why certain experiences have extraordinary impact.* Simon & Schuster.

Herculano-Houzel, S. (2016). *The human advantage: A new understanding of how our brain became remarkable.* MIT Press.

Isaacson, W. (2007). *Einstein: His life and universe.* Simon & Schuster.

Jiang, J. (2015). *Rejection proof: How I beat fear and became invincible through 100 days of rejection.* Harmony Books.

Kahneman, D. (2011). *Thinking, fast and slow.* Farrar, Straus and Giroux.

Levine, A. (2014). *On the edge: The art of high-impact leadership.* Business Plus.

Lewis, M. (2010). *The big short: Inside the doomsday machine.* Norton and Company.

Lewis, M. (2017). *The undoing project: A friendship that changed our minds.* Norton and Company.

Loomis, C. J. (2012). *Tap dancing to work: Warren Buffett on practically everything, 1966-2012*. Penguin Group.

Mackey, J., & Sisodia, R. (2014). *Conscious capitalism: Liberating the heroic spirit of business*. Harvard Business Review Press.

McDaniel, G., & Massen, S. (2017). *The dog's guide to your happiness: Seven secrets for a better life from man's best friend*. CompanionHouse Books.

McFadden, J., & Al-Khalili, J. (2014). *Life on the edge: The coming age of quantum biology*. Broadway Books.

McGonigal, K. (2012). *The willpower instinct: How self-control works, why it matters, and what you can do to get more of it*. Avery.

McGonigal, K. (2015). *The upside of stress: Why stress is good for you, and how to get good at it*. Avery.

Mlodinow, L. (2012). *Subliminal: How your unconscious mind rules your behavior*. Vintage Books.

Mlodinow, L. (2015). *The upright thinkers: The human journey from living in trees to understanding the cosmos*. Vintage Books.

Mlodinow, L. (2018). *Elastic: Flexible thinking in a time of change*. Pantheon Books.

Montague, R. (2006). *Your brain is (almost) perfect: How we make decisions*. Plume.

Mullainathan, S., & Shafir, E. (2013). *Scarcity: The new science of having less and how it defines our lives*. Picador Books.

Nye, B. (2014). *Undeniable: Evolution and the science of creation*. St. Martin's Press.

Nye, B. (2015). *Unstoppable: Harnessing science to change the world*. St. Martin's Press.

Nye, B. (2017). *Everything all at once: How to unleash your inner nerd, tap into radical curiosity, and solve any problem*. Rodale Books.

Oreskes, N., & Conway, E. M. (2010). *Merchants of doubt: How a handful of scientists obscured the truth on issues from tobacco smoke to global warming*. Bloomsbury Press.

Owsinski, B. (2016). *Music 4.1: A survival guide for making music in the Internet age.* Hal Leonard Publishing.

Ramachandran, V. S. (2011). *The tell-tale brain: A neuroscientist's quest for what makes us human.* W. W. Norton.

Randall, L. (2013). *Higgs discovery: The power of empty space.* HarperCollins Publishers.

Randall, L. (2015). *Dark matter and the dinosaurs: The astounding interconnectedness of the universe.* HarperCollins Publishers.

Rock, D. (2009). *Your brain at work: Strategies for overcoming distraction, regaining focus, and working smarter all day long.* HarperCollins Publishers.

Sapolsky, R. M. (2017). *Behave: The biology of humans at our best and worst.* Penguin Press.

Schroeder, A. (2009). *The snowball: Warren Buffett and the business of life.* Bantam Books.

Seung, S. (2012). *Connectome: How the brain's wiring makes us who we are.* Mariner Books.

Shermer, M. (2011). *The believing brain: From ghosts to gods to politics and conspiracies—How we construct beliefs and reinforce them as truths.* Times Books.

Schwartz, B. (2005). *The paradox of choice: Why more is less.* Harper Perennial.

Thaler, R. (2015). *Misbehaving: The making of behavioral economics.* Norton and Company.

Thaler, R., & Sunstein, C. (2009). *Nudge: Improving decisions about health, wealth, and happiness* (2nd ed.). Penguin Books.

Vance, A. (2015). *Elon Musk: Tesla, SpaceX, and the quest for a fantastic future.* Ecco.

Zander, R. S., & Zander, B. (2000). *The art of possibility: Transforming professional and personal life.* Harvard Business Review Press.

Zweig, J. (2007). *Your money & your brain: How the new science of neuroeconomics can help make you rich.* Simon & Schuster.

ABOUT THE AUTHOR

Alex Dontre is the drummer of the comedy-metal band Psychostick & adjunct professor in the Social & Behavioral Sciences division at Franklin University. Since 2000, Psychostick has released 6 albums & performed over 1,200 shows in Canada, England, Germany, Scotland, the (48) contiguous United States, Wales, & on one particularly metal cruise ship. In 2001, he received a black belt in Kuk Sool Won. He earned an A.A.S. in Finance in 2014 from Columbus State Community College, a double-major B.S. in Financial Planning & Financial Management in 2016, & an M.S. in Business Psychology in 2017, each at Franklin University. He continues to tour manage under the moniker "The Hammer" as well as perform & record with Psychostick.

www.ingramcontent.com/pod-product-compliance
Lightning Source LLC
Chambersburg PA
CBHW022208050726
47590CB00002B/700